THE RESILIENT TEACHER

Sarah L. Schlessinger

THE RESILIENT TEACHER

Creating Positive Change through Inclusive Classrooms

The Education Studies Collection

Collection Editor

Janise Hurtig

This book is dedicated to the people who have taught and continue to teach me about love.

First published in 2024 by Lived Places Publishing

All rights reserved. No part of this publication may be reproduced, stored in a retrieval system, or transmitted in any form or by any means, electronic, mechanical, photocopying, recording or otherwise, without prior permission in writing from the publisher.

The authors and editors have made every effort to ensure the accuracy of information contained in this publication, but assumes no responsibility for any errors, inaccuracies, inconsistencies and omissions. Likewise, every effort has been made to contact copyright holders. If any copyright material has been reproduced unwittingly and without permission the Publisher will gladly receive information enabling them to rectify any error or omission in subsequent editions.

Copyright © 2024 Lived Places Publishing

British Library Cataloguing in Publication Data
A CIP record for this book is available from the British Library
ISBN: 9781915734440 (pbk)
ISBN: 9781915734464 (ePDF)
ISBN: 9781915734457 (ePUB)

The right of Sarah L. Schlessinger to be identified as the Author of this work has been asserted by them in accordance with the Copyright, Design and Patents Act 1988.

Cover design by Fiachra McCarthy
Book design by Rachel Trolove of Twin Trail Design
Typeset by Newgen Publishing UK

Lived Places Publishing
Long Island
New York 11789

www.livedplacespublishing.com

Abstract

The work of teaching is nuanced, creative, and intellectual work, that is culturally undervalued. When that work is aimed at building inclusivity and social justice, it is often minimized or disallowed. This text offers narratives and practices for teachers for social justice and inclusivity to deepen their inclusive praxis for their students and simultaneously build the necessary resiliency to persist in doing the work. From curricular play to creating loving, trusting relationships with students, this book offers the stories of teachers who do their work brilliantly and, through their practice, sustain themselves and grow themselves in their profession.

Keywords

resilience; inclusivity; social justice

Acknowledgments

This text is a collection of narratives. Narratives are a fundamental way humans make sense of the world and share experiences. They help us understand complex ideas, emotions, and events by placing them within a relatable context. A narrative approach acknowledges that reality is multifaceted and offers a nuanced and comprehensive understanding of events or situations. A narrative approach also requires and relies on multiple perspectives coming together into one cohesive story. This is all to say that although my name is on the cover of the book, it only exists because of the thinking, teaching and contributions of very many people.

I would like to take this space to express my gratitude to those who helped create these narratives as I have represented them in this text. I am forever grateful to the individuals whose stories I share for their willingness to invite me into their classrooms, their thinking, and their hearts as we explored the complexity of teaching for social justice and inclusivity together. You are all actual heroes; you are brilliant, and I strive to be a little bit more like each of you as a resilient teacher.

The ideas that structure the analytic work in this text come from the many generative years of thinking, talking, and writing with Dr. Celia Oyler and Dr. Wanda Watson about a praxis of critical inclusivity, pedagogies of love, and how to prepare teachers who can pursue their social justice aims in the exclusionary context of our schooling system. Thank you to Dr. Srikala Naraian for teaching me what goes into the writing of a book and for always pushing my thinking with your thoughtful brilliance. Thank you to Dr. Kara Hollins for all of the impromptu reads of my drafted chapters. Thank you to Dr. Janise Hurtig; it has been a pleasure working with you and learning from you throughout the production of this text. And to the team at LPP, thank you all for finding me, trusting me, and for bearing with me through the growing pains of new parenthood. And, of course, thank you to Jamie for talking every little bit of this through with me and to Jude for giving me the absolute best excuse to not write.

Contents

Learning objectives   x

Chapter 1   Introduction   1

Chapter 2   Knowing your commitments   17

Chapter 3   Love, trust, and vulnerability   43

Chapter 4   Curricular play   65

Chapter 5   Loving learning communities   93

References   114

Index   121

Learning objectives

1. To understand the barriers to and complexity of teaching for social justice and inclusivity in a schooling system designed to sort and segregate.
2. To explore the power to build teacher resilience by teaching for social justice and inclusivity.
3. To consider the importance of a teacher's education and stance as they work to be resilient.
4. To confront and disrupt hierarchical power as a tool for building teacher resilience.
5. To embrace love and vulnerability as central components of teaching for social justice and inclusivity and of building teacher resilience.
6. To question curricular design and pursue responsive, accessible, and engaging curricular modifications as an act of teacher intellectualism and creativity.
7. To consider the importance of collaborative and loving learning communities for teachers' resilience.

1 Introduction

Changing the world is hard and so is teaching

I came to teaching by way of a commitment to equity. I grew up on the south side of Chicago in a neighborhood with a complex history around race and socioeconomics. My childhood neighborhood is home to a prestigious university that worked hard in the 1950s and 1960s to counteract white flight, and in doing so, created a space where racial and socioeconomic diversity were lived realities of daily life. That, coupled with my parents' efforts to make sure that, living on the south side of Chicago, I knew I was Jewish, led to a seriously skewed perception of US society. I was pretty sure that Chicago was a predominantly Jewish city (it is not), knew to stand for the singing of "Lift Every Voice and Sing" (the Black national anthem), and was well aware of my white privilege, even if I didn't have a name for it yet. My best friends and I all came from different family structures, different levels of wealth, and different racial and cultural backgrounds, and we all loved each other and shared our homes, families, and experiences.

I couldn't tell you what curriculum or textbooks my teachers were using, and I know that we were tracked for language arts and math. I know that the few white kids at the school were always in the "high-level" math and language arts classes. I also know that we studied W.E.B. Du Bois, and I assumed he was part of the national social studies curriculum until I got to graduate school. We took field trips to the Field Museum of Natural History *and* the DuSable Black History Museum and Education Center. We learned to care for each other: when it was time to take the Constitution test in eighth grade, we knew that Devon's learning disability was going to impact his success on the test, but there was no way that we were going to let him not pass. It's a sunny recollection of a place and time that were also fraught with tensions driven by that very same diversity. Nevertheless, this formative experience grounded me in a naive and unrefined but passionate belief that we learn from people who are different from us and that we all deserve equal access to opportunities to learn.

As an idealistic undergraduate student at a liberal arts institution, the one clear learning I could take away from my studies was that society was operating within and through biased structures that regularly created inequities. Our systems and standards created the haves and the have-nots. And more often than not, those structures operated on the basis of human difference, valuing particular differences as strengths and others as weaknesses. If a liberal arts education is designed to help students find their passion, Connecticut College had succeeded in its mission with me: I knew that whatever my work was to be, I had to work to change systems of inequity. I had to invest my life in making the world at least slightly fairer, and my theory was that the single most significant factor to invest in for a more equitable world was education. If everyone had access to excellent educational opportunities, anyone could develop the skills to change their own circumstances, they would have more opportunities to thrive, and if everyone had this access, everyone could succeed. Putting aside my obvious naivete regarding those very same systems I was sure I was going to change, this drive to provide equal access to excellent educational opportunities continues to be my driving motivation. It is a motivation that I share with the vast majority of teachers I have met across my 20 years in this field, especially when working from the most uninterrogated understanding of social justice: "'fairness' and 'equality' for all people and a respect for their basic human rights" (Sensoy and DiAngelo, 2017, p. xix).

My story is specific to me, but it is not unique. This commitment to equity and access are ubiquitous, although reached through a plethora of diverse lived experiences. Teachers, not all but most, come to the profession, as I did, because they want to make an impact. Those who come to teaching with social justice pursuits in mind generally want to make an impact for specific students regarding equity and access. On that path, they will likely deepen their understanding of social justice, as I did, encountering, recognizing, or being taught about the complexities and depth of our stratified society, the depth of this inequality in our daily lives and taken-for-granted ways of being, and the extent of the task and charge to make a difference (Sensoy and DiAngelo, 2017). They will encounter a great many frameworks to inform their mindsets and their practices, depending largely on the academic programs they enroll in and the academics that guide their introduction to the field.

Finding my commitments and my theorists

I first fell in love with the critical theorists like Jean Anyon, Paulo Freire, Henry Giroux, and Peter McClaren, who authored the texts that spoke to me in my undergraduate and early graduate career. Through critical theory, these scholars named the structures of society that were working to position some as "oppressed" and others as "oppressors" and offered critical pedagogy, a specific educational solution, as a path I might subscribe to in my pursuit of change. Critical pedagogy, they taught me, is grounded in the notion that teaching and learning are political acts and that we should all be given access to opportunities to question our world and to question power. As Giroux (2010) explains,

> Critical pedagogy opens up a space where students should be able to come to terms with their own power as critically engaged citizens; it provides a sphere where the unconditional freedom to question and assert is central to the purpose of public schooling and higher education, if not democracy itself. (p. 717)

This framework spoke directly to me and my democratic aims; it was about the political; it was about participatory citizenship; it was everything that I wanted to be enacting as a teacher. Until I learned more.

Geneva Gay and Gloria Ladson Billings brought culturally relevant and responsive teaching into my evolving framework. Their work helped me understand that a dominant white culture had set standards that were not reflective of the lives, knowledge, or experiences of people of color. They helped me see that, because of this white supremacy, school curriculum was inequitable and more accessible to white middle- and upper-class students than to students of color or students living under the poverty line. David Rose and Carol Tomlinson introduced me to concepts of Universal Design for Learning and differentiated instruction, approaches to designing and implementing instruction that would, potentially, make the lessons that I taught accessible to all of my students, even my students with disabilities. Teaching with a commitment to equity and access kept getting more and more complicated, and I hadn't even learned to question the construct of disability yet.

The reality of the classroom

I studied these scholars and strove to enact their philosophies and practices as I began teaching in a seventh-grade Collaborative Team Teaching (CTT) classroom. I traveled from classroom to classroom with my students, 50 percent of whom were diagnosed with learning disabilities, behavioral disabilities, and speech and language disabilities, as they received instruction in various standardized content. Time and time again, I found myself struggling, mostly with but occasionally against my co-teachers, as we tried to make the content "work" for this group of students. While all of my understandings of and commitments to social justice rang out loud and clear in my head and heart, the phrase "he just doesn't belong in this classroom" was the loudest sound of all. Recognizing that the "he" in this sentence was more often than not a male student and a student of color, I knew that I needed to dig deeper and understand why the Black and Brown boys were such a prevalent cohort in special education. I couldn't name what I saw, but I knew that it was something more complicated than coincidentally having multiple groups of students, year after year, where these "high incidence disabilities" were predominantly present in this particular cohort.

I knew that I was not supporting my students to access compelling learning opportunities or critical or responsive learning opportunities. Oftentimes, it felt like I wasn't helping them access any learning opportunities at all. As I sought to do better for my students and to understand what I can now name as the disproportionate representation of Black and Brown students in special education (Artiles, Trent, and Palmer, 2004), I found the scholars of disability studies and disability studies in education (DSE). By situating disability as socially constructed within our stratified society, by questioning who and what defined "good" or "smart," I began to see how disability as a difference continues to be seen as an individual human deficiency and a legitimate justification for exclusion in our society and schools (Valle and Connor, 2019). I also came to recognize how it is used as a mechanism through which to exclude people based on other markers of difference (Broderick and Leonardo, 2016) that deviate from a centered "norm," a white, affluent, male, cisgender, straight, English-speaking, Christian, and able-bodied "norm" (Garland-Thompson, 2017). Ferguson and Nusbaum (2012) offer that:

> the most important reason to explore the meaning(s) of disability is not to understand disability itself but to understand other categories of human difference. In

> other words, the study of disability (and the concept of "disability") is at the foundation of our understanding of the social construction of race, gender, class, and other ways in which we differentiate ourselves from one another. It Is essential, in short, to our understanding of how we see ourselves as same and different. (p. 73)

Difference was what mattered, or what we have made matter as a society. The societally constructed ways we value certain differences and vilify others have a real impact on people's lives, their access, and their opportunities. In disability studies in education, I found a philosophy that accounted for the inequities I was seeing and participating in across multiple intersecting markers of difference.

Finding inclusive education

I found inclusive education as the pedagogy that I could get behind to do the work of societal change. Inclusive education was somewhat of a revelation to me as I learned more about it. From a DSE perspective, inclusive education is not the service delivery model of inclusion, not my Collaborative Team Teaching class with students with and without labeled disabilities. Inclusive education is not a service delivery model, is not a place or location. It is a stance, an active pursuit,

> an ongoing struggle toward (a) the redistribution of access to and participation in quality opportunities to learn, (b) the recognition and valuing of all students' differences as reflected in content, pedagogy, and assessment tools, and (c) the creation of more opportunities for non-dominant groups to advance claims of educational

exclusion and their respective solutions. (Waitoller and Artiles, 2013, p. 322)

Inclusive education rejects inclusionism, which requires us to diagnose a person's disability, label them as different, push them out of typical classroom engagement because of that difference, and then allow them to be included in a general education classroom. Inclusive education instead embraces inclusivity, or "teaching all students, attending to the material needs of disability, and valuing all the differences in the classroom" (Schlessinger and Oyler, in press) full stop. I ground my commitments to teaching for social justice in a praxis of critical inclusivity, driven by critical disability studies and dis-crit and that is where I ground this book. In doing so, I hope to open the narratives and practices included to as many educators committed social justice pedagogies as possible. You have followed your own path to arrive at your commitments, and you may define them differently, but I hope to provide a space of connectivity where you know that you are not alone. I hope to support you to know that you are doing the work and that you can find ways to ignite and reignite your passion. This book is for teachers. You are resilient.

The struggle to teach for change

The work of teaching is nuanced, creative, and intellectual work that is culturally undervalued. To reach and teach a classroom of students well, a teacher has to know the students in the classroom, own the content and the formal curriculum, have enough confidence in their knowledge of the curriculum and of teaching and learning to manipulate the curriculum to be engaging for their specific students, know how to tell whether students understand the content, and know how to respond and adjust when they don't. All of this is done on a tight schedule with little room to "fall behind" the curricular pacing and while also holding the responsibility to "manage" their classrooms. If a student is struggling academically, that responsibility falls to the classroom teacher. If a student is struggling emotionally, that responsibility falls to the classroom teacher. If a student is struggling attentionally, that responsibility falls to the classroom teacher. All of these potential struggles of the individuals in a classroom, likely a classroom with too many students, impact the class as a whole and the learning that goes on within those walls. Teachers get to school before they can drop off their own children for the day. Teachers become team coaches and after-school tutors or simply stay after dismissal to get a handle on what happened that day and prepare for the next. Teachers bring work home with them, grading 30 plus papers overnight and planning class for the next day. Teachers fall asleep trying to figure out how to help that one student that they are so worried about, or what learning activity will actually help their students understand the learning objective. Teachers hold a responsibility to families; they are providing what are arguably the most important formative experiences to somebody else's babies. And don't worry, teachers have endless paperwork to stay on top of and are asked to cover other teacher's classrooms when they are absent to help out across the school. Nothing about teaching is easy. Maybe the summers, but summers are getting shorter and many teachers spend their summers in professional development, planning curriculum for the fall, or working a second job to make a little extra cash.

One would think that a career that requires this level of traditional knowledge, creativity, reflection, inquiry, people skills, research, organization, follow-through, and love would be highly valued, highly paid, and highly respected. While some cultures within our larger American society do position teachers as respected members of the community, the salaries and lack of autonomy associated with the profession tell a different story (see working a second job for extra cash noted above). Teachers hustle. They tutor, they scrounge for "per-session" pay through their school; I've even known people to keep their jobs with airlines or tending bar just to make it all work. Beyond the salary, rather than being exalted for the difficulty and complexity of the profession, teachers are infantilized for their choice to work with children and blamed and vilified for the flaws in a system they did not design and are often working to change. Drew and Sosnowski (2019) put it bluntly when they write:

> Many refer to education as the profession that eats its young (Halford, 1998). Nearly 50 percent of teachers entering the profession leave in the first five years (Ingersoll and Merrill, 2012). Attrition comprises 90 percent of the national annual demand for teachers, leading to a persistent shortage (Castro et al., 2018). Working conditions are cited as the primary reason teachers leave (Sutcher et al., 2016) (p. 492).

This is the general context of teaching. When a teacher is committed to building inclusivity and social justice, they are working under the burden of this general context of teaching AND grinding against traditional schooling systems that are built on principles of assimilation, standardization, and normalization which minimize or disallow social justice-oriented pedagogies. Teachers for social justice and inclusivity come to their work passionately and idealistically, eager to change a broken system built on underpinnings of white supremacy and ableism, eager to provide equity and access to their students. Whether it is the content that is taught, the ways of knowing and expressing knowledge that are privileged, or the behaviors that are deemed in/appropriate, teachers for social justice and inclusivity can see and feel the ways that traditional practices of schooling work to exclude and demoralize their students. They *want* to create change.

Managing the schedule and the responsibilities of teaching is a grueling task in and of itself. Doing so in a context that you are actively working to change can be overwhelming, disheartening, stressful, and isolating. Be it critical pedagogy, culturally sustaining pedagogy, anti-racist pedagogies, or inclusivity, all social justice-oriented pedagogies exist because the structures of schooling privilege certain people and oppress others. Teachers who come to know and love these pedagogies are committing themselves to being agents of change who can dismantle racist, classist, sexist, xenophobic, and ableist exclusionary structures (Ashby, 2012; Oyler, 2011).

I knew I was going to change the world from my position as teacher in my co-taught seventh-grade English Language Arts classroom. If I could reach all of my students, if I could find the right book to get each kid interested in reading, if I could create enough curricular space in the writing classroom to help them each find their voice enough to want to learn how to write … I believed that this work would make a change for my students and that change for my students would lead to a change for the school, for the next group of students, for every teacher who interacted with my students in eighth grade and high school. I knew that it would ripple. I knew my choices could create change. What I did not know or understand was that my agency, my efforts to make change, were contextualized by the resources I had, the policies and mandates of my school, the norms of teacher professionalism and student achievement, and the larger sociopolitical context in which I was working (Naraian and Schlessinger, 2021; Pantic, 2015). I knew that I could effect change, but I was not experiencing the change I wanted to see, and I internalized this as my own failure to reach my students and my own failure as an agent of change. And so, like so many others, I left the classroom seeking more knowledge to do better. In my case, I ran to academia. This frustration to do the work and make an impact, the tension between social justice-oriented pedagogies and the reality of school contexts (Naraian and Schlessinger, 2018) pushes many well-intentioned teachers to their limits, out of the field, or to abandon their ideals. I do not think it has to be this way. This book offers narratives and practices for teachers for social justice and inclusivity to support them as they work to build resilience, persist in doing the work, and grow their careers in the classroom.

White supremacy and ableism

In this book, I use the term "white supremacy" to talk about the systems of schooling that we often take for granted in the day-to-day of working in schools. When I use this term, I mean to refer to the complex and enduring systems of oppression that grant privileges to white people and disadvantage people of color (APA Task Force on Race and the Psychological Profession, 2017). White supremacy is rooted in historical power structures and continues to manifest through social structures, cultural representations, and economic policies (Sue and Spanierman, 2020). As Deliovsky (2010) argues, the very category of "whiteness" itself is a political construct used to justify the exploitation and marginalization of non-white groups for wealth, power, and psychological advantage. White supremacy can be blatant, like discriminatory laws, or subtle, like racial microaggressions, but its impact is undeniable, affecting everything from healthcare access to criminal justice outcomes and, of course, schooling (Jaffee and Casey, 2020). Understanding white supremacy as a system, not just individual prejudice, is crucial for dismantling its enduring legacy.

Ableism, a form of discrimination and oppression directed toward people with disabilities, is rooted in the assumption that people with disabilities are inferior or less valuable than those without disabilities (Goodley, 2016). Ableism can manifest in discriminatory attitudes, physical and social barriers, and societal expectations that exclude or disadvantage people with disabilities. It can limit opportunities for education, employment, and social participation, perpetuating a cycle of marginalization and inequality. Annamma et al. (2013) highlight how "racism validates and reinforces ableism, and ableism validates and reinforces racism" (p. 6) through their parallel and intersecting systems of oppression. Throughout this book, as I refer to white supremacy and/or ableism, I do not separate the two as distinct systems of oppression. As I refer to teaching for inclusivity and for social justice, I am forwarding the belief that in order to dismantle white supremacy, we must also dismantle ableism, and in order to dismantle ableism, we must also dismantle white supremacy.

Resilience

Teacher resilience can be understood as the "capacity to manage the unavoidable uncertainties inherent in the realities of teaching" (p. 39) and to "maintain equilibrium and a sense of commitment and agency" (Gu and Day, 2013, p. 26). It is the ability of teachers to cope with the challenges of the teaching profession and to continue to be effective in their work. Resilience is not survival; it is more than survival. Survival suggests just making it through, sacrificing what you need to, keeping your head down, taking one day at a time, getting through the job. Resilience, on the other hand, is powerful. Resilience is the continued pursuit of commitments and goals, the continued confidence to advocate and push forward deliberately, even when it is a challenge, even when you get knocked down. Resilience is what it takes to work toward social justice and inclusivity day after day in the contexts of systems of schooling and societal constructs that perpetuate exclusion and inequity.

Resilience is not something that you can expect to find innate within yourself, nor is it a "capacity" that we can test for. It is situational and dynamic, shaped by personal experiences and contextualized (Mansfield et al., 2016). A commitment to teaching for social justice and inclusivity is one of those factors that shapes resiliency. On the one hand, working against societal structures to effect change can create more barriers for a teacher in the daily practices of their job. On the other hand, it is this same commitment that can be drawn on as a resource to build resilience. The same thing that creates those barriers can be used as a mechanism to foster your resilience. I left the K–12 classroom after five years. I did not know how to draw on my commitment to equity and access to deepen my resilience. I have spent the years since then learning from teacher after teacher about their practices for social justice and inclusivity. I have watched their resilience grow. It is their stories that I want to offer you as you seek to build your own resiliency by/while teaching for social justice and inclusivity.

A caveat

It shouldn't be this way. To work this hard, this thoughtfully, and against so many taken-for-granted structures; to work with this much love and receive so little in return; it shouldn't be this way. This book is not intended to give the educational system validity or to suggest that this is what teachers should have to do in order to teach for social justice and inclusivity. Nevertheless, this is the system we have inherited. This book is for those people who are not Ok with this system and who want to try to change it, even knowing how much uphill work there is to be done. There may be moments in this book where you feel yourself getting angry and wondering why you should be asked to do so much extra just to do your job. And you are right. It isn't fair, but it is the reality of this work. My hope is to give you some tools to manage it and do the work that you are passionate about. The key to resilience lies in understanding the importance of being realistic at the same time as being aspirational. This means acknowledging the current situation for what it is while still holding onto our goals for the future and for change.

Each narrative in this book is intended to highlight a particular practice of inclusivity that built teacher resilience for people like you. These practices intersect and overlap. They are also challenging and can take years to build into your practice. Take what is useful for you here, what feels like it will help you, and keep your focus on the purpose. You want to make change and you don't want this system to push you out. This is who you want to be, so let's help you be that teacher, that person.

2
Knowing your commitments

Teacher education programs aimed at graduating social justice-oriented educators tend to start their programming with a reflective moment for student teachers to consider who they are and what informs their decision to teach. These programs will then go into the foundational theories that guide the program's approach to teaching for social justice and inclusivity. Professors ask education students to reflect on their personal histories through the lens of these theoretically driven programmatic underpinnings. For example, student teachers might be asked to read portions of Kendi's (2023) *How to Be an Anti-Racist* and then discuss or write about their own biases or the ways in which they do or could begin to speak out against racism. They may be assigned chapters from Valle and Connor's (2019) *Rethinking Disability: A Disability Studies Approach to Inclusive Practices* and use a social model of disability framework to revise previous statements they made about teaching and learning or their ideal classroom. The learning theory behind this approach suggests that we must begin to teach for social justice and inclusivity by naming the systems that oppress and seeking to understand the ways in which we are complicit in that oppression through our mundane, everyday actions (Oyler, 2017). It suggests that we must first reflect on and reframe our social justice commitments to make intentionally inclusive social justice-oriented decisions in our teaching practice. So much of what school is and what school does is taken for granted. So, in order to understand how to teach inclusively, how to be a social justice-oriented inclusive educator, it matters to understand the ways that schools and pedagogies are and are not working toward those same goals.

I met Catherine[1] when she enrolled in one of these teacher education programs aimed at graduating social justice-oriented educators who teach inclusively. In many ways, her choice to enroll in this particular program already illustrated that she had a commitment to teaching for social justice and inclusivity. Born and raised in New York City, Catherine, a Latina woman, had grown up through schooling that she could name as exclusionary. In her own schooling experience, she had seen how students who spoke multiple languages were positioned as "low-performing students" in classrooms that privileged the reading and writing of the English language. She had experienced her own family being alienated during parent–teacher conferences. And she had felt her own pushout when she began receiving speech services out of the classroom and regularly missing class content.

Catherine studied education and philosophy during her undergraduate career and came to her new teaching career and graduate studies ready to discuss structural racism, xenophobia, and ableism. Even with this in-depth experiential understanding of

1 The names used in this book are pseudonyms to ensure the anonymity of the participants.

exclusion in schools and a foundational exploration of theories that push back on structural racism and ableism, Catherine spent her early years in the classroom uncovering and unpacking the exclusionary context and practices of schooling. This chapter focuses on how Catherine learned to use her commitments to social justice-oriented education and inclusive teaching to consistently question, reflect on, revise, and reinvigorate her practice. Catherine's experience is a testament to how teachers can use the critical skills of questioning the taken-for-granted practices of their classrooms and schools to build their resilience as they navigate and work to change those very same exclusionary practices.

Catherine's commitments

One of the most challenging parts of learning to teach inclusively as a social justice-oriented educator is unlearning our own experiences of the classroom. For many of us, school was a place where students sat at desks while teachers gave lessons from the front of the room. We were expected to sit quietly, raise our hands, ask permission to do anything, and complete work in our workbooks or from our textbooks. It was the students' job to pay attention, read closely, write clearly, and ultimately get the correct answer without looking for it in the back of the book. Unfortunately, this structure does not account for the vast variability in the human experience (lived, cultural, physical, or neurological). Consequently, it sets up a hierarchy that privileges particular people's ways of knowing and being over others'. Students who do not sit quietly or who struggle to write clearly are made to feel that they do not belong in the classroom, that they are not good students, that they are not smart people. Teaching inclusively means empowering teachers to build classroom spaces where all students across the vast range of complex lived, cultural, physical, and neurological differences can feel that they belong, are participating members of the classroom community, and get to learn. Yet, because this is not how so many of us experienced school, because we often take it for granted that school needs to look still, sound quiet, and result in accurate completion of tasks, it can be quite easy to fall back into these hierarchical and exclusionary habits of being.

Catherine had experienced pretty traditional and, for her, exclusionary schooling. Consequently, as a student teacher, she immersed herself in an exploration of inclusivity that asked her to question these practices of schooling, whom schools were designed for, and whose knowledge and experiences were left out or pushed out. In studying the social model of disability, she had learned to understand disability as a social construct, meaning that society imposes barriers that make it more difficult for some individuals to participate in school, work, and the general activities of daily life (Valle and Connor, 2019). For example, we take it for granted that sidewalks should and do have curbs without considering how those curbs make it difficult for people with mobility impairments to access sidewalks and streets. Catherine believed that it was her job as an inclusive educator to remove unnecessary barriers to her students' participation in her classroom curriculum. This meant that she wanted to focus on her practice and how she created opportunities for all of her students to participate and learn rather than focus on individual student's disability labels. She had also learned quite a bit about the racist foundations and structures of American schooling (Love, 2023). Much like the physical barrier of curbs, the metaphysical barrier of whiteness meant that curricular content and teaching approaches were often designed in ways that excluded Black and Brown students from full participation. She wanted to focus her teaching practices on centering and affirming all students' cultural and linguistic identities in her classroom (Paris and Alim, 2017).

What is more, she had learned about the intersection of race with disability and how a disproportionate percentage of Black and Brown students were labeled with disabilities and put into segregated special education service delivery models (Artiles, 2019). From this perspective, Catherine built an understanding of the ways that ableism and racism worked together as oppressive systems, but also how special education could actually work as a mechanism of segregation and remediation (Connor et al., 2016). In her own practice, she did not want her students pulled out for interventions or put into groups determined by "ability" because she did not want to limit any student's access to the community or the curriculum.

In translating these theories into practice, Catherine was committed to using a Universal Design for Learning (UDL) framework (cast.org), building a trusting classroom community (Sapon-Shevin, 2010), and understanding student behavior as communication (Greene, 2014). She knew that by focusing on the tenets of UDL and designing lessons that provide multiple means of engagement, representation, and expression across her curriculum, she could ensure that all of her students were participating in and learning from classroom activities. She also knew that if she spent time building a positive classroom community where students trusted her and each other enough to take risks and support each other, the academic learning they could do together would be rich. This same community would also allow her to differentiate her supports for each student without evoking shame or questions of fairness from her students. She knew she needed to view her students' behaviors as a form of communication, reflect on her perceptions of particular behaviors as good, bad, or disruptive, and support her students to learn behavioral skills that positively served them and their classroom community. Not only had Catherine studied these ideas, grounded in her philosophical commitment to social justice-oriented education and inclusivity, she had practiced them. She had crafted and implemented a universally designed unit as a student teacher. She had been part of a trusting and supportive classroom community. She had worked with students to build collaborative and proactive solutions to problems that were triggering their challenging behaviors and helped them be more productive members of that community. Catherine clearly understood her commitments to social justice and inclusivity, the educational theories that supported them, and some practices she could use to pursue those commitments. She was ready to bring her idealistic and impassioned self to the real world of teaching.

Commitments contextualized

Catherine took her first full-time position at a school she knew had a reputation for being committed to social justice and inclusivity. Some of her classmates had completed their student teaching at the same school and had spoken highly about their experiences. So when Catherine got the school's offer to be the special education licensed half of a fifth-grade co-teaching team, she was elated. The student body of the school was approximately 30 percent Latinx, 30 percent Chinese, 30 percent Black, and 10 percent white. A public school, it was also socioeconomically and culturally diverse, and many students in Catherine's class spoke multiple languages. Catherine's classroom was an integrated co-teaching model, meaning that about 50 percent of her students had diagnosed disabilities. In her case, this included children with diagnosed Intellectual Disabilities, Specific Learning Disabilities, and Other Health Impairments. The school's general approach to teaching this diverse population was to leverage small-group work. Her students all engaged in benchmark assessments at the beginning of the year and were sorted into small groups for reading, writing, and math instruction. For each teaching period, the whole class would receive the same lesson, and then they would break up into small groups for differentiated practice. Catherine and her co-teacher would work with their assigned groups across the week to support the group of students in completing each day's learning task.

At first, Catherine felt great about her classroom and her practice. She was teaching a diverse student body where students with labeled disabilities were taught alongside their same-aged peers; she got along well with her students and they respected her; she worked well with her co-teacher; and the classroom generally ran smoothly. As she settled into the routine, however, she began to notice a few things that weren't sitting right with her. For example, their literacy curriculum was centered around a class text that they read and discussed together. Usually, her co-teacher would read the text aloud, stopping along the way to ask students questions about the text. Then the class would break up into small groups to continue their engagement with the text and write short responses to teacher-created questions about the book. Catherine and her co-teacher were each responsible for supporting three of the six small groups. They had created groups based on students' reading levels as determined by the benchmark assessments that they took at the beginning of the year. Because of her special education background, Catherine had been given the responsibility of supporting the two groups of students who had scored lowest on their benchmark reading assessments and then a third group of students who had scored second highest on those same benchmarks. The co-teaching team's rationale was that Catherine could focus on providing the most intensive supports to the lowest-performing students and then would have a third group that did not require as much time or attention. Her co-teacher, on the other hand, could focus her energy on supporting and extending the learning of the top tier of students as well as monitoring any less significant needs of those students in the middle-tier groups.

The structure was logical on its face, but as Catherine lived through it, she could feel it not working for her students. Her two groups of students with the most significant needs seemed to be relying on her guidance to do any work at all, rushing to complete work, and disengaging from the whole-group read-aloud and small-group work. As her students disengaged, they completed less work or did not do it with any real understanding. This created a downward spiral. Catherine's small groups were not prepared for or were not able to participate in the next day's lesson and read-aloud. Her students were falling more and more behind as the book and the formal curriculum moved forward. Being behind then, of course, led to less engagement and more behavioral problems from these two groups, which also meant Catherine needed to give them more of her time and attention. Her top middle-tier group was not getting any of her attention at all, and she could see them starting to disengage as well. Dragging the class through the book and the short response questions in small groups was becoming Catherine's most dreaded 45 minutes of the day.

These are the moments that can pull teachers down and push them out, because they are not just moments. They become the entire tenor of the day, the week, and eventually the job. The rhythm of time spent knowing students are not learning, feeling frustrated by student behavior and disempowered by a test-driven curriculum works on teachers day in and day out and can take away the desire to teach. This feeling of futility is not what anyone wants when they sign up to teach, especially if they intend to teach for social justice. Yet, the structures around teachers can feel impenetrable. I have heard too many educators acknowledge the disconnected nature of a standardized test-driven curriculum and then follow that acknowledgment with phrases like, "But that's what they need for the test, so what can I do." Disempowered teachers just keep doing the same thing, and students do their best to stay present. When students fail or cannot force themselves to sit still while teachers deliver content in inaccessible or uninteresting ways, we blame the children, we blame families, and we blame colleagues. And our own frustration grows.

What stands out about Catherine is that she did not ignore this moment. Instead, what she did became the foundation for the longevity of her career. She paused. Catherine felt herself dragging, her frustrations with her students, their families, her colleagues, and herself growing. But she did not push through. She paused, and she looked backward to look forward.

Theorizing the taken for granted: Acknowledge and investigate

When Catherine hit her moment and pushed pause, she started by simply acknowledging to herself that what had seemed like a logical structure was simply not working for her, her co-teacher, and most importantly, her students. Her students' work, their behavior, and her own misery were enough evidence for her to know that even if this path did result in passing standardized test scores, it would also likely create negative academic self-concepts for her students. They were starting to share the feelings that they "just weren't good at school," and it was breaking her heart. Her teaching was sending these young people the message that they were not capable. It was a bitter pill to swallow, accepting that *her work* was causing the exact thing she had come to teaching to change. But there it was. She still had that original underlying commitment to teaching for social justice and inclusivity, and she knew that she was not enacting that commitment in her daily practice. Social justice and inclusivity. That was why she was here to begin with, and she needed to get back to that. So she swallowed her pill and began to investigate why her approach wasn't working. Not knowing exactly where to start but remembering how passionate and capable she had felt coming out of her student-teaching experience, she began by looking back to what she had learned as a graduate student in order to decipher how she had strayed so far from her intended path.

During her graduate studies, Catherine had been particularly excited by the educational theories that had informed her experience as a student teacher. Disability Studies in Education (DSE) had helped her name that there was no such thing as "normal" and that exclusion and inequities persisted because so many social systems were designed around a "normal" center that did not include her or her students. Critical Race Theory (CRT) had pushed her to really see how whiteness was the guiding force of that "normal" center and how these social systems worked to perpetuate power and systems of oppression. Disability Critical Race Theory (DisCrit) brought into focus the ways that racism and ableism worked together to justify these oppressive systems. Each of these frameworks had previously helped her refine her commitment to social justice and practices of inclusivity. Each framework also highlighted that this centered "normal" was deeply taken for granted and that working to change it required consistent and deep reflection (Paris and Alim, 2017). That is where Catherine had lost her way. She hadn't given up on her commitments; she had just been swept away by a system that makes oppressive and exclusionary choices seem natural and that kept her too busy to question her choices.

Fortunately for her, because these theoretical frameworks that had fanned her passion all posited that deep reflection was a key component of employing them for any practical purpose, they all also offered questions through which to reflect. Catherine pulled five major points for reflection from DSE, CRT, and DisCrit:

- Question your curriculum
- Question your assessments
- Question your classroom community
- Question the role of power
- Question your advocacy

Using these overarching themes and questions from her peers, mentors, and the academic scholars she admired, she started to dig. She wrote about these questions, she talked about these questions, she alienated her co-teacher with these questions, but she kept digging. In her excavation, what she uncovered was how quickly she had fallen back into systems of oppression without even realizing it, and some excitement at the prospect of changing it up.

Question your curriculum

To refine her understanding and her thinking about her curriculum through a DSE/CRT/DisCrit lens, Catherine asked herself:

> "How does my curriculum challenge or reinforce dominant narratives about disability and Whiteness as social constructs and their roles in shaping educational knowledge?" (Artiles, 2010; Delgado and Stefancic, 2023; Ladson-Billings, 2014)
>
> - Am I actively challenging ableist and Eurocentric perspectives and narratives and incorporating diverse perspectives and voices from marginalized communities, including histories of resistance and counternarratives?

- Do I center my students' experiences and voices, recognizing and valuing their lived experiences and cultural knowledge as legitimate sources of knowledge?
- Do I provide opportunities for students to develop critical thinking skills and question dominant narratives and power structures?
- Do I challenge deficit models of disability and emphasize the role of environment and societal barriers?"

When Catherine reflected on these questions, she unearthed some significant taken-for-granted ways of being in school that she was promoting in her practice. Specifically, she did not feel that she could answer a single one of these questions in the affirmative. She was not incorporating diverse perspectives from marginalized communities or centering her students' experiences or voices. She was not providing opportunities for students to think critically; in fact, she had created learning experiences that required students to tell her the "right" answer. She was not challenging deficit models of disability or working to mitigate environmental and societal barriers; instead, she was ignoring that print text can often present as a major barrier to learning/participation, and she was unintentionally locating this issue within her students' current reading abilities rather than within her instructional design. Across her curriculum, she wanted to rethink a lot of things, but that felt really overwhelming. Panic attack-level overwhelming. She took a deep breath and tried to determine what one thing here was the most important for her commitments. She couldn't narrow it down to just one, though, and instead decided that she needed to start by rethinking the way that she and her co-teacher were choosing class novels to read and rethink their practices that privileged print text over all other ways of learning and knowing.

Question your assessments

To refine her understanding and her thinking about her assessments through a DSE/CRT/DisCrit lens, Catherine asked herself:

> "How do my assessments and learning outcomes promote disability justice and racial equity?" (Paris and Alim, 2017; Waitoller and King Thorius, 2016)

- Are my assessments culturally and linguistically responsive, avoiding biases that disadvantage students with disabilities and/or students of color?
- Are my assessments accessible and inclusive, avoiding assumptions about what constitutes "normal" or "appropriate" learning?
- Are accommodations readily available and provided without stigma? Do activities consider sensory, cognitive, and physical differences?
- Do I offer multiple pathways for demonstrating knowledge and understanding, recognizing and valuing different forms of expertise and expression?
- How do I ensure that my grading practices and feedback mechanisms are fair and equitable and do not disadvantage students based on disability or other intersecting identities?
- Do I actively question which demonstrations of learning are interpreted as "smart" and which are interpreted as "struggling"?

Again, here, she could immediately feel herself cringing at how far off the mark she had been in her practice. She felt positive about her grading practices, and she was not going to stop using benchmark assessments to understand her students' reading strengths and needs. But she knew that, for example, only using writing to assess student learning was exclusionary and biased. She knew that she was centering traditional academic forms of expression as superior or more "appropriate" than others that might be more accessible, familiar, or engaging for her students. She knew that using benchmark assessments as a singular mechanism to determine the makeup of small groups was creating a hierarchy of "smartness" and that, while the purpose was to provide "struggling" students with accommodations, these accommodations were consequently stigmatized and attached to "good" and "bad" academic identities. She was definitely committed to using small groups but simultaneously intimidated by the complexity of changing the grouping structure. The challenge was also exciting, though, and she knew that a high-leverage move like this could change the entire vibe of her classroom.

Question your classroom community

To refine her understanding and her thinking about her classroom community through a DSE/CRT/DisCrit lens, Catherine asked herself:

> "How do I create a classroom environment that is welcoming, anti-racist, anti-ableist, and inclusive of all students while promoting critical consciousness about race, power, and social justice and celebrating diversity?" (Slee, 2013; Tatum, 2017)

- Do I actively cultivate a sense of belonging and community where all students feel valued, supported, and empowered to fully participate?
- Do I encourage open communication and collaboration, allowing students to advocate for their own needs and preferences?
- Do I foster open and honest dialogue about racism and ableism, creating a community that helps students feel comfortable sharing their experiences and perspectives without fear of judgment or marginalization, while also encouraging students to critically examine their own biases and assumptions?
- Do I challenge microaggressions and promote open dialogue about cultural, racial, and neurodiversity within the classroom community?
- Do I actively question which behaviors are understood or interpreted as "good" and which are understood or interpreted as "bad"?
- Do I collaborate with special educators, disability service providers, and student support services? Am I open to learning from and involving students with disabilities in shaping the learning environment? (Biklen and Burke, 2006; Slee, 2013)

When it came to this question, Catherine felt pretty positive about much of what her practice was. For example, she did believe that she was questioning herself when she felt like a student was behaving in an antisocial or disruptive way. She would always ask herself if the behavior was actually disruptive, or if she was just interpreting it that way because she did not like the behavior. Rather than labeling the behavior as "good" or "bad," she would always ask herself what the behavior told her about the student and their needs and what replacement behavior she could possibly teach them (Greene, 2014). Catherine also knew that she had made good use of her school's morning meeting space to actively cultivate a sense of belonging for all of her students. That allowed them to have open communication and even address cultural and neurological diversity. She had relied heavily on resources from *Responsive Classroom* (https://www.responsiveclassroom.org) and *Morningside Center for Teaching Social Responsibility* (https://www.morningsidecenter.org) to plan this portion of the school day, and her students were developing real relationships with each other and trust in her. Still, she saw things in this area that she could work to improve. She didn't want her community building to be limited to morning meeting and then for its meaning to disappear for the rest of the day. She wanted to work to bring these key features of belonging, openness, and communication into the more academic moments of the day as well to build her students' sense of self, courage, and criticality.

Question the role of power

To refine her understanding and her thinking about the role of power in her school and classroom through a DSE/CRT/DisCrit lens, Catherine asked herself:

> "How do I challenge and disrupt the reproduction of Whiteness and other forms of systemic privilege and power within my classroom environment and interactions?" (Apple, 2000; Dei and McDermott, 2014)
>
> - Do I examine my own implicit biases and how they might influence my interactions with students and pedagogical practices?

- Am I mindful of the power dynamics within the classroom and how my position as an educator might impact student experiences?
- Do I encourage students to engage in activism and advocacy, both within and beyond the classroom, to address issues of injustice?
- Do I model critical engagement and social responsibility in my own teaching and interactions with students and colleagues?"

Catherine knew that she was always thinking about her own implicit bias; her graduate program had done A LOT of work around implicit bias. She was struggling a bit to understand if [determine whether?] her implicit bias was influencing her interactions with her students and her pedagogical practices. She decided that she needed to do more reflection for herself around her implicit bias as it connected to her pedagogical decisions. In considering how to do this, she realized that she was relying uniquely on her own brain and experience for too much of her teaching and reflection. The power dynamics within her classroom were such that she wasn't eliciting enough opinions from her students to know their experiences. As a new teacher, she was intimidated by going to her colleagues for their perspectives. She thought they would likely judge her for her lack of knowledge or, worse, for her "idealism". She realized that she needed to move away from her independent reflection and find more community with her students and colleagues to think through these big questions. She added this goal to her ever-growing action plan and moved on to her final set of reflective questions.

Question your advocacy

To refine her understanding and her thinking about how she was advocating for her students through a DSE/CRT/DisCrit lens, Catherine asked herself:

> "How do I advocate for systemic change within my school and community to dismantle barriers and promote disability justice in education?"
>
> - Do I speak up against discriminatory policies and practices that disadvantage students with disabilities?
> - Do I collaborate with disability rights advocates to promote systemic change and create a more equitable learning environment?
> - Do I model inclusive practices and disability awareness for colleagues, administrators, and the broader community?"

Catherine's reflection here was a little murky. On the one hand, she knew that she did speak up against evidently discriminatory policies. She was, in fact, quite proud of herself for that, especially given her status as a novice teacher in the building. Still, she was realizing through all of her other reflection that there were many discriminatory policies that she hadn't seen or named for herself. She was only beginning to understand that she needed to advocate for systemic change for her students. To complicate things, she was also realizing that in some instances it felt like the only way to advocate for her students was to leverage their disability labels, which felt contradictory to her DSE commitments. Her students needed resources, interventions, and supports, and not advocating for those would be wrong, but she did not like how it felt to use a deficit model of disability to acquire those resources and supports. With this reflection, she mostly felt lost and confused.

Act from reflection

Through this deep self-study, Catherine unearthed a multiplicity of ways that she was not doing the work she had intended to do and not honoring her commitments to social justice and inclusivity. Some of her reflection was disappointing to her, some was confusing, and some was sparking her passion. While this may read as even more discouraging and daunting than the futility and tedium she had felt before her reflection, in actuality, Catherine was psyched. She was amped up. First of all, her reflection had unearthed systemic issues, structural barriers to her students' engagement and success. And while that was, of course, disappointing, it was also comforting to reframe the issue and take the onus off of her students and off of herself. What is more, the reflection didn't just help her reframe the issue; it got her thinking about actions she could take to make change. The wheels were spinning as she thought about ways to center her students' voices and disrupt hierarchical power, to bring the spirit of their morning meeting community into flexible grouping strategies during academic periods, and to make all of her content more multimodal. She knew that as she got started on this work, she also had to find ways to grow her reflective community. If anything, she had too many ideas she wanted to work on or try. The amount of work to do may have been intimidating, but it was also invigorating. Her passion for effecting change was regenerative

Over that year and the years to come, Catherine made many changes to her curricular designs, her assessments, and the way she built and relied on community in her classroom. Sometimes, she argued with administration, and other times, they praised her for her innovations and engaged students. While they did not always sanction her approaches, they were delighted when her outcomes matched their espoused social justice goals. This is not a narrative that ends with Catherine finding a solution for how to teach inclusively. Later chapters in this book go more in-depth on the changes that teachers make to their classroom practices in order to teach for social justice and inclusivity and how those changes and practices fuel their own resilience. Although I could tell you those parts of Catherine's story too, what stands out about her, what I hope you take away from this narrative, is how she used her commitments to social justice and inclusivity to pull her out of the ickiness, tedium, and disillusionment that can push teachers out of the classroom. To this day, Catherine would tell you that she is still learning how to teach inclusively and teach for social justice. And if you sat down for a cup of coffee with her, you would be sure to hear about her latest deep dive into whether a practice is best serving her students or not. You would also likely notice the passion in her voice, the curiosity she has for your opinion, and the excitement vibrating through the air if she lands on a change she could make or a plan she might try. Catherine continues to turn the seeming futility of struggle against an exclusionary and oppressive system into her passion through reflection on her commitments, and it keeps her in the classroom working for change.

Commitment to yourself is a commitment to your self

Those teacher education programs aimed at graduating social justice-oriented educators who start their programming with foundational theories to guide a pedagogical approach will tell you that educational theory matters for classroom practices. They will tell you that these reflective practices matter to check your implicit bias and to not harm children through the enactment of oppressive practices. And this is all true. Reflective practices grounded in well-aligned theory are essential for teaching for social justice and inclusivity. What you might not learn in those programs, and what Catherine's story highlights, is that reflecting on your practice through and with the theories and frameworks that align with your commitments can also be instrumental in building your own resilience. Doing this work of teaching for social justice asks us to be altruistic, to be activists, but it also requires us to take care of ourselves.

In her book *Onward: Cultivating Emotional Resilience in Educators* (2018), Elena Aguilar speaks directly to the need for all teachers to work diligently to care for themselves. She argues that the demanding nature of teaching, coupled with external pressures, can leave educators feeling overwhelmed and unfulfilled. She then offers a practical road map for cultivating resilience and reclaiming the joy of teaching with an emphasis on prioritizing self-care and self-compassion. Catherine's story highlights that self-care for educators who are teaching for social justice and inclusivity is inextricably intertwined with attending to the commitments to social justice and inclusivity that brought them to the field in the first place. Reflecting on your practice through the lens of the theories or frameworks that underlie your commitments is an act of self-care. It is attending to your passions and aligning your choices and actions with what truly matters to you. By reflecting and pursuing your pedagogical commitments with dedication, you acknowledge your own worth and invest in your own growth and happiness. It's a powerful form of self-love that can translate into increased confidence, refined practice, and resilience in the career.

Building Resilience from Commitments

Why did you start teaching? What are the articles you have read, the podcasts you have listened to, and the TED Talks you have watched that had you nodding your head and annotating with a simple "yes!"? Who are the professors, teachers, colleagues, and classmates that have inspired you throughout your education and career? If you think you might be in need of some self-care by attending to your pedagogical commitments, these resources are your starting points:

1. **Collect your resources:** Your passions have origins and inspirations. Collect those resources to remind you of why you are here in the first place, to pull you back into your idealism. Catherine used her coursework and me, a former professor and forever colleague in the field, to help her collect her resources.

2. **Refine your resources:** What are *your* top five most significant themes that come from the resources that you collected? The top five most important to you and your passion and your reason for teaching. Use the resources that you

collected to make those top five themes extremely clear for yourself and create questions to ask yourself about them. Oftentimes, education authors have put questions or practices at the end of their articles. Use those. If you happen to be fueled by DSE/CRT/DisCrit, use Catherine's questions if you want. Or ask AI to help you create some reflective questions about your themes. Catherine didn't have AI, so she used me and her former classmates to start, and with time, over the years, creating and refining reflective questions has become second nature to her.

3. **Investigate:** Use your questions. Write about them. Video journal about them. Talk with your colleagues, your spouse, your students, and your administration if you are feeling brave. Use your community and the learning power of social interaction to dig deep into your practices and your pedagogical decision-making through these questions that capture your passions and commitments as a teacher for social justice and inclusivity. You will uncover some disappointments and hit roadblocks, but push through to the generative side of these conversations. Don't stop or give up when you hit the phrase "but we have to prepare them for the tests." Remember that year-round test prep is never the answer and let yourself get excited about creative possibility.

4. **Act From Reflection:** Your investigation and reflection will be generative. You will have ideas that come from your writing, talking, and collaborative thinking. You might have more than you can manage, like Catherine did, or you might have only one or two. Either way, start with one action that is realistic and that you know will move your practice into alignment with your commitments. See how that one

small action impacts your practice, your mood, and your investments.

5. **Don't Stop:** You may make one small move; you may make many huge moves. You may create a tiny spark or ignite a blaze. Wherever you land, remember that self-care requires attending to your passions. Don't stop after one move. Make it a weekly practice to check in with yourself and your commitments – Are you attending to your passions? What is the impact on your practice? Take care of your educational passions.

Knowing your commitments curricular extension

Collect your resources: Your passions have origins and inspirations. Collect those resources to remind you of why you are here and ground you in your idealism.

Think back on your life in and out of school. When you think about being a teacher working for social justice and inclusivity, what texts inspired you along the way? Think about texts broadly – books, articles, podcasts, television shows, films, even a conversation you had. Go back to old syllabi or old emails. Use the chart below to start to collect your commitment inspiration.

The text (book/article/podcast/film)	Who created it?	Who brought it into your world?	Why do you love it?	Quotes or other authors/educators named in the text.

- Notice if there are specific content creators who stand out to you, and put a star by their work to remind you to look them up and find their new work.
- Notice if there are quotes or other authors/educators that you want to know more about, and put a star by their name.
- Notice if there is a theme that stands out from your inspiration and write it below:

3
Love, trust, and vulnerability

At the heart of teaching for social justice and inclusivity lie strong relationships and a vibrant classroom community. This is no mere feel-good add-on. As Bettina Love writes, "Relationships are the oxygen of social justice education" (2019, p. 12), the very foundation upon which critical learning and transformative action can flourish. Without trust and a sense of belonging, students cannot feel confident to engage with the vulnerability and risk-taking that criticality and deep learning require. These relationships cannot be superficial, aimed at control and achievement, but must instead be humble and human, aimed at knowing and learning with our students (Valenzuela, 2010).

Building these vital connections takes intentionality and effort. It starts with educators fostering an environment where diverse voices are heard and where students' identities and lived experiences are valued, centered, and celebrated (Muhammad, 2023). It requires the disruption of power within classroom spaces and teachers' critical reflection on "ways their own interpretations of classroom policies and practices perpetuate interactional and systemic oppression" (Annamma and Morrison, 2018, p. 75). It requires love and the perspectives and care that humanize students (hooks, 2003). When surrounded by peers and educators who value their voices and experiences, students feel empowered to learn and empowered to act. This same foundation of love, care, and shared experiences can also be instrumental for teachers in building their resilience.

This chapter explores Grace's attention to love, trust, and vulnerability in her fourth/fifth-grade split classroom. I begin by describing what a loving, trusting, and vulnerable classroom space can look like and how these practices informed Grace's passion and resilience as a teacher. I then offer some suggestions about where a teacher might begin their own work building love, trust, and vulnerability in their practice to teach for social justice and inclusivity while also building their resilience.

Embrace difference

> Relating to children as human beings who are working with what they have to seek happiness, approval, redemption, joy [...] accepting that they might seek those feelings through acts of violence, anger, hurt, and revenge [...] I can facilitate the growth of children as individuals with specific histories and experiences rather than as receptacles for my own values and ways of knowing.
>
> – Grace

In our classrooms, no matter how homogeneous we imagine them to be, there are innumerable differences, ranging from the mundane to the profound. For many educators, talking about differences, especially those that divide our society and that have been used as oppressive tools, is a nonstarter. But if we ignore difference, when we pretend it is not there or does not impact us all, we eliminate the beauty and growth that come from varied experiences being shared, celebrated, and put into collaborative action together (Lorde, 1997). Worse, we are telling our students that they cannot trust us; that they cannot act with vulnerability because we do not love them; that we want to ignore them and their complex identities; that we are afraid of the difficulties that engaging with our differences might evoke. To love our students is to see them entirely for who they are and to value their unique identities. Without this, they cannot trust us, and they certainly cannot be vulnerable.

Grace is a white, Queer, presently able-bodied, culturally Christian, Cis Woman from the Pacific Northwest of the United States. Grace's engagement with how her identity was taken up and pushed out by her community and her family has set the stage for her to understand why embracing the differences that constitute students' identities is necessary for educating for social justice and inclusivity. She knows firsthand how it feels to have parts of her identity ignored, to be pushed out, or to be told she does not belong because of who she is. She is also keenly aware that her own experience does not make her an expert on the experiences of others and that societal structures, schooling structures specifically, work to make some markers of difference more complex for individuals to engage with openly and vulnerably. For example, her Queerness, while central to her own identity, is not a visible marker of difference in the way that race is, and therefore identifying as Queer and identifying as Black are not comparable, even though there are shared experiences of push-out and exclusion.

For Grace, learning is deeply intertwined with trust and vulnerability. In order to learn, we must be willing to take risks, fail even (Varenne and McDermott, 2018), and learn from the outcome of our risks, successes, and failures. It is significantly more approachable to take risks and be vulnerable when surrounded by people who love you and have shown you that they appreciate your whole self. That requires that educators "build honesty in low-stakes places – nothing is shameful – but you have to do it first. You have to be honest all of the time. Constantly actually sharing yourself." Working from this belief, Grace has crafted a complex collection of content and practices to honor her students for their differences and build a community that sees and values each other, where her students can take risks and learn deeply.

For example, Grace designs content for her fourth and fifth graders to directly engage with issues of race and power in our society. Her unit on the Roots and Branches of Power was an interdisciplinary unit exploring race in contemporary US history, specifically looking at performative speech as a tool for social justice. She curated a variety of texts, including speeches, music, poetry, and sermons from the civil rights movement, and had her students work to analyze the texts, questioning the roots of power. Having carefully chosen texts that students would recognize and others that would be new for them, Grace ensured that the content spoke to the complex intersection of struggle and joy that characterizes Black American History (Muhammad, 2023), and the students were able to critique and name oppression while also celebrating a rich and vibrant cultural history. They individually analyzed the authors' language choices, why particular choices spoke to them, and what they thought any underlying meanings of the language choices might be. They then worked to find shared themes across their individual analyses. In her racially diverse classroom, this opened the metaphorical door for all her students to consider their personal cultural histories. They began contributing to the classroom text sets with music, speeches, and sermons from their own lives across various racial and cultural differences. As they listened and listened and listened, they annotated, questioned power, shared from their worlds, spoke to oppression, celebrated joy, and honored each other's full identities within their academic classroom context.

Collectively honoring the numerous differences in academic and social contexts in Grace's classroom builds a foundation for Grace and her students to create from difference and problem-solve across difference. Working with identity and building language to speak about identity and difference throughout the school year, her students have created art installations that showcase the literal tapestry of their identities, worked to petition for changes in exclusionary school policy, and found ways to bring their conversations beyond themselves, beyond their classrooms, and even beyond their school, out into the community. Talking openly about identity also leads to a "community built on trust so we have a foundation for the community to solve a problem."

While this work is intended to support students in their learning, it also supports Grace's humanity and her resilience as a teacher. She learns from her students and grows her understanding of the world through their willingness to share. She gets to experience a classroom fueled by student interest, support for each other, and celebration of each other. She has a community of people with whom to solve classroom problems. She thrives on the love she builds for her students and the love they all cultivate for each other. When the external pressures of her school around testing achievement or curricular expectations might weigh on her, she has a community of support that engages and excites her thinking right there within the classroom because she has invested in them.

Disrupt the hierarchies, share the power

> I build a house I want to hang out in and need help putting it together. It's not just mine; I want to live in it with my companions, sharing the labor and delight of it.
>
> – Grace

On the first day of school at *School for the Community*, teachers have already been hard at work organizing their libraries, arranging their desks into collaborative groups, and decorating their bulletin boards with bright and inviting schedules and posters. Grace has been hard at work, too, but you would not know it from the look of her classroom. The desks are piled in one corner along with their chairs, and beside them are some empty bookshelves and stacks of so many books. There are bins of various sizes and colors in the center of the space. The closets are open and filled with piles of cardboard, bags of textiles, bottles of paint, tape, markers, sentence strips, and more school supplies than you can imagine. There are a few empty easels, and the bulletin boards are brown and bare. You might think that the teacher in this room had gathered everything a classroom would need but did not have enough time to put it all together, and you would be partially correct. Grace has put specific and intentional effort into gathering the materials she knows that her classroom and her students will need in the coming year and organizing those materials to be visible by category as students walk into the space. However, she never intends to set up beyond that initial collection of materials because this classroom is not hers. It is all of theirs, hers and her students', and they will spend their first weeks of school collaboratively designing their space, learning how to share their ideas, and coming to a consensus as they move bookshelves and a rug into a reading nook, find a way to section off a peace corner, or create resource centers for writing and math materials.

Grace's intention with this practice is multifaceted. She wants her students to have ownership over their shared space and feel empowered to move through their classroom independently with clear knowledge of where to find the resources and materials that will support their thinking, learning, and producing across the year. She wants them to create the spaces that they know they will need to focus academically and to feel safe emotionally. She wants them to know they are a community where all their opinions and ideas are valued. She wants them to learn to share those ideas, listen to other ideas, and make compromises and collective decisions. And she wants them to wonder why this teacher is letting them make these decisions. They will not trust her on that first day or maybe even in that first month, but this move is intended to invite them into a trusting relationship with her.

For a teacher to relinquish the design decisions of their classroom is an act of bravery, and from day one, Grace wants her students to know that she believes in them and trusts them to make decisions for themselves and the collective. She positions herself as a consultant to them. She provides structures for conversations that she facilitates, during which the students learn about accountable listening, about managing disagreement, and about building consensus. She is present and available for questions as the children move through the classroom, usually in self-selected teams, designing, organizing, and creating. They come to her with disagreements that they need help to solve or questions that they have about the task. At first, the students ask questions intended to elicit their teacher's approval, confirming that they are doing it the right way. Over the week, though, as Grace responds with trust in their decision-making and questions to prompt them to continue to problem solve, the students' questions become more exploratory, more adventurous, and even wacky. They become more reflective of who these students are and what their creativity and imagination can do. Curricularly, this first week's work will evolve into the maker space Fridays that the students will enjoy all year. Philosophically, it grew from Grace's commitment to building genuine and meaningful relationships with and among her students. Relationally, it sets the framework for a classroom community of people who will be brave together, take risks, share their experiences, and trust that they will be heard and respected.

Why does this practice matter so much? Why does it have such a significant impact on the students in Grace's classroom? Many students, even those as young as nine, have only ever experienced school as a controlling space. If students want to move their own bodies or speak, they have to obtain permission. The teacher is responsible for assigning work and asking questions, and the student is responsible for completing that work, regardless of their interest in or dis/connection to the content. That work is then evaluated by standards set by the teacher, and yes, there is a "right" way and a "right" answer. When it comes to the power structures of schooling, students can almost always be found at the very bottom of that hierarchy. These practices of control tend to be more intense and restrictive in schools in underserved communities. Research has shown that schools that predominantly serve students of color tend to employ more carceral practices (Love, 2023). Students with disabilities are only allowed to participate in school based on their proven readiness for the least restrictive environments, implying that restriction is a necessary component of teaching students with disabilities (Taylor, 2004). Students of color and with labeled disabilities are often very used to highly restrictive environments that limit them in how they move their bodies, what content they are allowed to engage in, and how they are allowed to participate. Frequently, students have no opportunities to share their voices and experiences or think and act critically. The teacher holds the power, and the students must defer to that power. Students become a guarded school version of themselves with walls and self-employed coping mechanisms to protect themselves from the disempowerment of schooling.

Grace's classroom set-up practice explicitly and intentionally disrupts that power hierarchy. That makes this practice, or others like it, very uncomfortable for students and teachers. Grace's colleagues have called her a "free spirit," among other things, for using practices like this. And for as much as she is committed to this work, she will also admit to some fear every year as students make choices that she thinks are absurd. But, as Grace and her students move through the discomfort of disruptive work together, as her students push their limits with her and test their boundaries, as she shows them time and again that they are part of their own development, they become willing to step out of their carefully constructed school versions of themselves because she has stepped out of hers. This classroom co-design is one piece of many in disrupting the hierarchies that work to exclude students and toward empowering all students to voice their perspectives, challenge dominant narratives, and promote equal participation. Relinquishing power and inviting shared ownership over design demonstrates to Grace's students that she is doing more than talking the talk.

While disrupting hierarchical power structures in the classroom is a dynamic, if scary, practice of teaching for social justice and inclusivity, it also has a powerful impact on teacher resilience. By inviting her students to share in the design of their classroom space, Grace not only positions them as her partners, building their sense of self, she also creates space for 28 contributing thinkers for her own work and design. Collaborative learning contexts and experiences lead to shared responsibility for knowledge transmission. This curricular context allows Grace to learn from her students and adapt and grow as a thinker, educator, and human, even as she supports their learning. There is collective care for the classroom space and community that rejects notions of traditional classroom management and relieves Grace of the stress and responsibility of controlling 28 other people all day long. Through shared decision-making processes, Grace limits her teacher-decision-making fatigue. What is more, the increased student engagement and the thoughtfulness with which the students take care of each other, their shared spaces, and their responsibilities are an actual delight for Grace as their teacher. Shared responsibility, opportunities for her own personal development, and experiences of joy and delight directly reinforce Grace's commitment to her students and to her work as a teacher. They build her resilience.

Listen to students

> If they don't feel like they can speak in front of other people in the room or be truthful because they're afraid, then it's harder for them to do the work. And the more personal they're able to get with the academic content, the deeper their thinking goes.
>
> – Grace

Grace and I joke about the experienced teachers' keen ability to hear the difference between the sound of "productive chaos" and "just plain old chaos." While I do believe that there might be something to that skill, the joke is premised on the idea that learning can be a noisy business. It is from the noise in our classrooms, the voices of our students, that we can begin to know them, understand them, and respond to who they are. Cultivating a classroom environment where students feel heard and understood is crucial for fostering positive learning experiences. Students feel valued and respected, which, in turn, increases motivation and engagement (Fredricks et al., 2019). When teachers listen to their students, they gain valuable insights into individual experiences, needs, and challenges inside and outside of the classroom, academically and social-emotionally (Weinstein et al., 2018). Listening to students from diverse backgrounds allows educators to develop culturally responsive spaces that value and celebrate diverse experiences (Gay, 2010).

The key to this practice of listening, however, is developing a context in which students feel safe to speak. This is particularly difficult to do because traditional schooling structures have taught us that the student's place is to listen. It is even more challenging to do when working with students from underserved communities who have been made to feel "other" or "less than" for sharing their experiences or opinions or simply for being in their own bodies within a school building. The magic of this practice, however, is that once students believe that they can share without negative ramifications, they really do share, and they tell you how it is. Once Grace's students believed that she was, in fact, a trustworthy adult, they would tell her everything from when they thought her assignments were not the best to when they were managing trauma at home:

> I mean they would make fun of me for losing my glasses all the time and made it a classroom job to find them. Lukas told me that he thought I was probably overwhelmed by the class (I was). Kids come out to me all the time. Anne wrote me a note telling me that she didn't feel like she had a racial identity Not white enough not Asian enough.

Active listening and responsive listening in action

The willingness to share is directly reciprocal to the responses students receive from their listening teachers. Like many elementary teachers, Grace holds a daily morning meeting in her classroom. She also has reflective journals for her students and often builds a community council among them. In each of these practices, she invites her students to share their feelings, ideas, and opinions. The work of listening then comes in, not in the assignment or activity for the students, but in the response to what they share. For example, Grace likes to start her morning meetings with a practice called "clearing." Sitting together on a rug in the front of the classroom, students share one by one what they are feeling and what their emotional needs are for the day. "Clearing" is intended to help all of the community members be in positive relation to one another and offer or ask for support from each other. For students who feel comfortable or at least perform comfortably in this practice, Grace has easy access and insight into how to support them through their learning that day.

Kai, Grace's student, resisted participation in this part of the community meeting. A fourth grader in the fourth/fifth-grade split classroom, he would climb under a desk off to the side of the group and engage himself in some other activity: under-desk pull-ups, sketchbook drawing, staring off into the distance. When he was coerced into staying with the group for "clearing," his sharing was always limited to a quick and straightforward "I don't know." Then Grace introduced the option of sharing your feelings through visuals, shapes, and drawings. Given this option, when it came his time to share, Kai told the class that he felt like a "black hourglass." Grace was sure she did not know the meaning of his imagery, but she held his eye contact and thanked him for his contribution. Over time, Kai continued to share the black hourglass image. And one day, before the morning meeting even started:

> he came to school and held up a note to me, saying "I'm not talking today Grace." I responded by thanking him for letting me know, and that sometimes we don't feel like talking, which is fine. When the children came to the rug for Morning Meeting, Kai brought several sheets of paper with him, and when it came to his turn in the clearing, he held up his drawing of an hourglass. I asked Kai if I could explain so that the others knew what was happening. He held up a sign he had made that said "OK." I explained to the others that Kai didn't feel like talking today, so he would respond to them in writing instead. There was little reaction from the students, this seemed to make sense. Later, during independent reading, Kai approached me with another sign, which said, "There is a reason I don't want to talk." I told him that I had figured he had a good reason, and I trusted him to tell me about it if he needed to, and that I was there to listen (or read) if he wanted to share. He held up his "OK" sign and went back to his seat. A few minutes later, he approached me with a sign saying "My uncle is dying of lung cancer." I put an arm around him and told him I was sorry, that this was a hard thing he was going through, and thanked him for telling me. I let him know that we could talk more if he needed to. We stood there

for a moment side by side, and then he held up his "OK" sign and went back to his seat. Within the hour, he had begun speaking to his friends and appeared more relaxed. He didn't come back to me after that, but the next day when he came to the rug for morning meeting, he had his hourglass sign again. He was talking that day but used his image rather than his voice to share his feelings.

After this exchange, Kai began to participate in "clearing" and in morning meetings in more overtly participatory and meaningful ways. He no longer hid himself away under a desk as his classmates shared about their needs, and although he stuck with that black hourglass sign for a long time, he eventually began to share other dimensions of his emotional state and needs.

It mattered that Grace:

1) Held a specific moment in the day to engage in listening;
2) Centered that moment around student participation rather than her own agenda; and
3) Actively responded to what her students shared with her.

She listened to Kai's self-segregation and responded by including alternative ways to share. She listened to Kai's visual symbol and gave it respect as she sought to better understand it. And she listened to Kai's expressed need not to share and gave him the space to quietly be with his own emotions. As a result of all of that listening and responding through clear and relatable actions, Kai began to choose to share and be heard. What is more, Grace listened to Kai's "way of sharing/knowing feelings and imagine(d) other children's access points as more complex than (she) had previously considered." It also made her consider her own emotional responses and question whether she herself was "always willing to make my feelings accessible to others? What value does that have? When is it helpful? If I am honest, it doesn't always feel safe for me to share my feelings truthfully." From listening, she was able to be responsive to the needs of her students and herself and to create practices within "clearing" and morning meetings that invited multiple ways of sharing without requiring it.

Listening beyond the morning meeting

Grace does not limit her listening to morning meetings. Her daily instruction always includes small-group and independent work time, but rather than focusing on her students remaining quiet and still during these working blocks, she focuses on making sure that they know she is listening. She sits with them in groups without guiding conversations and checks in on them one-on-one to learn more about their thinking and processes. She positions herself, once again, as a consultant in the space and teaches them that they can come to her and ask for support. She has them keep a section in their journals called "Notes to Grace" that she checks daily and responds to both in writing and through responsive actions. It can look and sound messy and loud, even chaotic, but it creates a context for the organic sharing of ideas, challenges, experiences, and emotions.

When a student mentioned in passing that she was upset that they were not doing anything to reflect on 9/11, Grace responded by shifting their social studies unit to ground it in current events as they relate to the events of September 11, 2001. When her students told her that they did not feel like they knew enough about that tragedy or current events to create a strong mapping of connections, she leveraged their desire to know in order to teach them about developing strong research questions and research practices. She created the context to hear her students, listened to what they had to say, and took action to respond to what they shared. And through her responsive listening, she continued to build their faith in her and their willingness to share with her and with each other.

Again, this practice is mutually beneficial to Grace and her students. As Grace's students feel heard, they engage more deeply with classroom content and in a loving relationship with their teacher. As a teacher, Grace is then able to design more engaging learning experiences and to feel closer to her students. School can be a place for her to watch people she cares about learn things. School can be a place where she can engage her creativity in response to her students' ideas. When her voice is not the loudest or the only one that matters, being in the classroom is exciting, invigorating, and challenging, which is motivating for her as an educator.

Developing practices that foster resilience through love, trust, and vulnerability

Grace has been working as an upper elementary teacher for 16 years now, and she certainly did not start her first year of teaching with her classroom unfinished or by exploring the complexities of race and power in American society. These are practices she has built over years of teaching, practices that she continues to refine. Grace came to her teaching with a commitment to the power of community.

> This commitment comes from the culture of my family, and also religion, to be always caring for other people and helping and giving what you have. It's like that churchy life, that hippie churchy life, but it's also for me in reaction to abandonment, and rejection, and the harm of that same framework. Both of those drive that connection making, building community, putting people together, helping.

She has used that commitment to build and rebuild, make and remake, content and practices that speak directly to identity and embrace difference, disrupt traditional schooling power hierarchies, and help her listen. But that wasn't overnight work. Each of Grace's practices that I highlight in this chapter started as a small idea, a glimpse into a possibility. Over time and iteration, they have evolved and continue to evolve.

In no way do I imagine any teacher reading this chapter and replicating Grace's practices, but instead taking inspiration from them to consider where they might deepen their own practices around building trusting community and relationships in their classroom. Just as Grace recognized the uniqueness of each of her students, each teacher will be unique in how they embody love, build trust, and share vulnerability. To that end, the call is to develop a process for developing your own practices to build a loving community that supports you and your students.

1. **Start with your commitments:** If you are not committed to real love, trust, and vulnerability, you will not do the work, or at least not well. So consider: Why does it matter to you to create classroom communities of love and trust? Maybe those concepts don't work for you, but you want to focus on positive teacher–student and student–student relationships. Why? And in what ways? Ground your work in a true commitment, and it will feed you.

2. **Be open to possibility:** The number one barrier I encounter in my work as a teacher educator and teaching consultant is, simply, the current reality of our schools. Too many of us see things the way they are and do not believe that pedagogies of love, trust, and vulnerability will be allowed. But what if they were? What if you tried something small, and it went well? What if you could support it with research from the field and data from your classroom? Be open to the possibility that things can change.

3. **Identify possibilities:** Start small. Consider where you could embrace difference, disrupt power, or be a responsive listener with your students. Consider other ways to build trust and love that I have not written about here. Recognize your discomfort with these ideas or the vignettes above and ask yourself what makes you un/comfortable. What are your boundaries on control? Why? What are your boundaries on bringing your whole self and sharing honestly with your students? It took me 15 years of classroom teaching before I felt comfortable sharing my Queer identity with my students, and I had good reason for that fear. I also saw my practice and my students' response to me change dramatically once I made the decision to be fully myself in the

classroom. Where can you push yourself to add to the curriculum, respond to a student, or let go of your control? List your possibilities and try one small thing.

4. **Trust your students:** Without fail, when teachers give their students some space to be in charge of themselves, within clearly defined boundaries, students rise to the occasion. They might need time to push limits and see how you respond. It might take time for them to step into a decision-making position. Trust them. Give them a chance. Kindergarten through high school, they can and they will step up to the challenge if you give them the chance, the boundaries, the support, and the respect.

5. **Document everything:** or rather, empower your students to document everything with you. Curating your work and theirs provides you with the data to build your small move into something a little bigger and a little bigger. It also provides you with a lens to look back at the work your community built together and glory in it, critique it, build from it, reuse it … whichever practice(s) motivate you as a teacher.

6. **End-of-day sifting to make sense:** When you have charged yourself with responsively listening to students, spaces become honest and raw; when there is a cacophony of voices creating the community, it gets complicated and overwhelming. Save space and time for yourself outside of the classroom and away from students to debrief the day, sift through the moments, and consider what needs further attention. It does not hurt to do this work with a co-teacher or friend if that is available to you.

7. **Iterate:** One small relinquishment of control might feel great. What could it look like to grow from there? One practice for responsively listening might fail on its initial trial. What can you learn from the failure and change in your practice? This work is extremely complicated and will never be a one-and-done practice. Entering into it with the idea that it must be iterative and responsive to your own growth and to each new cohort of students you teach will sustain the practice over time.

Love, trust, and vulnerability curricular extension

Identify possibilities: Start small. Consider where you could embrace difference, disrupt power, or be a responsive listener with your students. Where can you push yourself to add to the curriculum, respond to a student, or let go of your control?

Video analysis can help us see what we cannot see in the moment. Record video of a concentrated teaching block where you can clearly see yourself and your students.

1. Watch your video one time through looking for moments when you are in power or assert power. Note those moments.
2. Watch your video a second time through looking for moments when a student or students assert power either as anticipated or as resistance. Note those moments.
3. Pick one moment of teacher power and one moment of student power that you would like to explore in the context of this chapter.

Teacher power moment

What was the teacher move in this moment?

What was the purpose?

Was it about maintaining your comfort/control or facilitating student learning?

Would there be potential value in disrupting this dynamic?

What could that look like?

Student

What was the student move in this moment?

What might the purpose have been?

Would there be potential value in disrupting this dynamic?

What could that look like?

4
Curricular play

> Curriculum is the centerpiece of educational activity. It includes the formal, overt knowledge that is central to the activities of teaching, as well as more tacit, subliminal messages – transmitted through the process of acting and interacting within a particular kind of institution – that foster the inculcation of particular values, attitudes, and dispositions. (Bayer and Liston, 1996, p. xv as quoted in Sleeter and Carmona, 2017, p. 12)

Curriculum means many things to many people, from the strikingly technocratic formal curriculum purchased by your school that prescribes what you should say and do for each day of the year, to the deeply esoteric curriculum that is the ever-present teaching, learning, and construction of knowledge we engage in simply by being in the world (Black Paint Curriculum Lab, 2024). For the purposes of this book and to support the resiliency of teachers working for social justice and inclusivity, I will rely on Walker and Soltis' (2004) perspective on curriculum, which offers that curriculum encompasses the entirety of the educational program, including the following:

- **Purposes**: Why are we teaching this? What are the goals of education?

- **Content**: What knowledge, skills, and information will students learn?
- **Activities**: How will students engage with the content? What learning experiences will they have?
- **Organization**: How is the learning program structured and sequenced?
- **Null:** What content and experiences are entirely absent from the educational experience? What topics, historical events, cultures, or perspectives are not covered in the curriculum?
- **Hidden Curriculum** (Apple, 1976)**:** What are the unwritten, unofficial lessons and messages students learn in school beyond the formal curriculum? What implicit values, norms, and expectations permeate the entire school environment?

(Walker and Soltis, 2004)

From this perspective, curriculum is not a fixed entity and certainly not a neutral or objective one. It is not just a written document outlining topics to be covered. Instead, it is a dynamic process that unfolds within the classroom through the interactions between teachers, students, and the learning environment, carrying the complexities of difference, power, and knowledge in every layer of the content. Teachers and students shape the curriculum together, consciously and subconsciously. Even when there is a formal document with standards, scripts, and a pacing guide, the way the teacher presents that material and the way the students engage with or resist those experiences all constitute the curriculum of the classroom. Curriculum resides in the shared experiences of the classroom and the knowledge constructed therein.

The past decade has witnessed a significant shift in the educational landscape regarding curriculum. Once dynamic and shaped by individual educators and local contexts, formal classroom curricula have become increasingly prescriptive in response to the rise of standardized testing and a pervasive audit culture. The relentless pressure of high-stakes standardized testing, designed to measure student achievement in core subjects and attached to school funding and failure, has imposed a focus on a limited range of skills and knowledge. Educators, facing pressure to improve test scores, are often left with little choice but to adhere to prepackaged curricular materials and rigid pacing guides aligned with the test standards. This leaves little room for creativity, in-depth exploration of subjects, or for tailoring instruction to meet the diverse needs of students. School systems are increasingly subject to external scrutiny, unannounced school visits, and data-driven accountability measures. This focus on quantifiable outcomes creates a climate of fear and compliance, pushing educators to prioritize test preparation over fostering a love of learning and cultivating critical thinking skills.

Increased reliance on standards-driven, scripted curricula and testing practices is, not surprisingly, more prevalent in underfunded, underserved communities and neighborhoods. In an effort to close the so-called achievement gap, policymakers and school administrators have focused their efforts on supporting students in performing better on standardized assessments. In doing so, they have neglected to consider the racial and cultural biases of these high-stakes tests (Asera, 2016) or the limiting educational experience for students who only receive skill-and-drill teaching to prepare them for test taking (Bailey and Oyler, April 1, 2024). When "testing season" comes around, teaching for social justice and inclusivity can feel impossible. What is worse, for many schools, "testing season" has become the only season, and there is no curricular space left for criticality, creativity, or joy. This repetitive, dull drum creates a malaise for students and for their teachers. Curricular content that is less and less engaging, accessible, and responsive (Waitoller and King Thoruis, 2016) creates uninvested students who demonstrate their boredom and discontent in a range of complicated and often difficult ways (Annama and Morrison, 2018). This, in turn, creates a teaching population that is, frankly, miserable about going to work where they have no opportunity for creativity or excitement and where they are often managing complex behavioral issues that result from a disengaged and rightfully resistant student body.

In this chapter, I share the stories of three educators experiencing the impact of "testing season" and its broader curricular weight. For Luz, Nia, and Klaudia, the only way to navigate the restrictive curricular requirements of their schools while holding to their commitment to socially just and inclusive education was to find ways to play with the curriculum that would increase student engagement while also attending to administrative requirements. In this curricular play, they each found practices and strategies that engaged their students and a delight and passion within themselves for employing their own creativity and resistance to strengthen their resilience.

Learn from one to teach for all, leverage all to teach for one
Luz

Over her ten years of teaching, Luz had developed a belief in "the importance of social-emotional development in the early childhood classroom and throughout children's educational lives." This stated belief was evident in the design of her kindergarten integrated co-teaching (ICT) classroom space, complete with emotional support teddy bears and a quiet corner. Luz was distressed that her students, upon leaving her kindergarten classroom, whether with or without individualized education programs (IEPs), would no longer be allowed to play, cry, and be emotional beings but would instead be required to sit, "behave," and take tests. Although first-grade students were not required to take state exams, the impact of the testing culture was such that in Luz's school, students began to practice for state exams in first grade. She worried about how quickly her students might be told they did not belong in these ICT and general education settings.

As a kindergarten teacher and one who believed so sincerely in the social-emotional development and support of all of her students, Luz felt alienated in a school that, from her perspective, privileged and prioritized testing over students. She felt disempowered by her conversations with the administration and her colleagues, who insisted that students must begin to prepare for state exams as soon as possible. Luz was bothered by the abrupt educational change that her students would inevitably experience when they transitioned into first grade and felt that the school culture would not change in response to her beliefs or her students' needs. She decided that her only course of action was to be realistic about what was within her locus of control and act from there. She could not change the way her school prioritized testing, but she could play with her own classroom curriculum. She decided to reconsider her curricular design in order to support her students in engaging in the kind of academic expectations of the first-grade classroom but with the social-emotional supports she had mastered in her kindergarten. She explained to me that:

> I feel like if we limit the kids to just reading, writing, and math, we're going to have so many more kids that are frustrated and don't want to try anymore. If we give those kids that are having trouble with reading, writing, and math other opportunities to learn and feel successful, I'm sure their reading, their writing, and their math would get better too.

She believed that "teaching them these things here [in her kindergarten classroom] when they are safe, they have choice, and they are playing" could help prevent students from becoming lost, falling behind, or being moved to more restrictive environments in the coming year when they would spend the majority of their days sitting at desks.

Use data to know your students

Luz wanted to create a thoughtful, student-centered, and emotionally supportive curriculum. She decided to focus on math because she was the most unsure of her own instruction in this content area. Typical math instruction in Luz's kindergarten classroom included a short mini-lesson with the whole class wherein they would all practice counting or review emergent concepts of addition and subtraction. Station or center learning then followed, with students working in groups of three to four on varied learning activities to support their development of the skills and concepts associated with the unit's mini-lessons. Working in independent groups or with the support of a teacher or paraprofessional, students would work through specific math tasks, using manipulatives and writing or drawing representations of their work.

During these sessions and upon a review of student work, Luz noticed that Melissa, Eduardo, and Byron seemed distracted or confused. They did not seem to be participating orally during whole-group instruction or small-group work. Their written work often did not follow the task directions, and it seemed as if the adults in the classroom were dragging these students through completing the work rather than having them engage with the activities in a way that would support their learning.

Luz decided to start with case studies of these three students, Melissa, Eduardo, and Byron, whom she had identified as "struggling" with mathematical foundations. All three of these students had IEPs or were in the process of being evaluated for a disability. She knew that all of her students would be expected to enter their first-grade classroom with at least good number sense and counting skills. She worried that these three students, in particular, would be pushed out into more restrictive settings if they could not perform on the first-grade benchmark assessments. She also knew that working to meet the legal requirements of their IEPs gave her a point of leverage to support her curricular play.

She began by observing Melissa, Eduardo, and Byron during daily choice time. Byron was a fan of dress-up and the blocks and of finding hiding places. Melissa was really into the Abiyoyo[2] story and would spend her choice time writing books about herself and Abiyoyo. Eduardo liked to play with dinosaurs and could often be found drawing them. Luz recorded video to see how her students responded during whole-class lessons. She took photos of them engaged in station activities and collected student work. Using all of these data, Luz was able to make sense of the spaces and activities where her students were already using math concepts, and the spaces and activities where she could provide more support.

Add, subtract, or modify

Luz played with her curriculum to offer more whole-group instruction through mini-lessons that specifically addressed the academic needs of these three students through the kind of play and joyful interactions that they were accustomed to in her classroom. For example, she observed that her students were having a hard time with mathematical language like "putting together" and "taking away." Using what she knew about Melissa's interest in storytelling and Eduardo's love of all things dinosaurs, the kindergarten class acted out a play together during multiple mini-lessons. In the play they were all dinosaurs, and they were being

---

2 Abiyoyo is an African-folk-tale-turned-children's-book about a giant that terrorizes a village.

"put together" and "taken away." As they reenacted this activity through a story that Luz told, the students practiced counting all of the dinosaurs as a whole and as they were "put together" and "taken away." Luz also began to use large gestures to signify "put together" and "taken away," gestures that she then practiced and reinforced with her students at their centers and in other daily activities. For example, at the end of the day, as students left the classroom in small groups, Luz would count with the students how many people were left and would "ask Byron 'did we just put together or take away?'" and then wait for Byron to "say 'take away' and make the hand motion."

Luz also began to develop new tasks at differentiated math centers, having her students complete work reminiscent of the first-grade test prep curriculum but through activities that drew on their joys. For example, she considered the expressive language she had heard Melissa using in her retelling of the Abiyoyo story and designed a math center where students created their own math stories to tell each other and would draw representations of each other's stories. She strategically grouped students so that they could work together and support each other and engage in the activities that would be most accessible and appropriately challenging. This ensured her an opportunity for one-to-one instruction and small group support. In doing so, Luz was able to have her entire kindergarten class happily engaged in the classroom activities while also demonstrating mathematical understanding that would show up in the testing expectations of their first-grade classrooms.

How it turned out

Through this work, Luz felt affirmed that she was supporting her students and that she was being the educator she wanted to be. She knew that her curricular choices supported the developmental needs of *all* her students – academic and social-emotional – and that they would all be able to engage with the testing that was coming their way. To be clear, her goals were not about testing or preparing her students for a standardized exam; they were about protecting her students from the harm that the future exam was poised to visit upon them if they were not given an opportunity to be successful learners first. By working from the needs of a few to design something that worked for the whole class, Luz was able to create an inclusive curricular space that provided opportunities for learning and success in school for all of her students. It also gave them the foundational skills to be successful in less inclusive spaces.

While these types of wins are not systemic overhauls, they are wins nonetheless. Luz felt confident that she had done right by her students. She felt invigorated by enriching and growing her practice. Making these curricular moves empowered her to stay at her school for a few more years, share her practices with the larger community, and push to change the culture around teaching and learning in the early elementary years. She was able to share her success with her kindergarten students to help other educators in the early elementary classrooms consider less restrictive ways they could engage their students in learning. In this way, she leveraged her whole class's success to help the school create more inclusive classroom learning for other potentially marginalized students.

Ultimately, Luz determined that working to change a school culture was more than she could sustain in the long term. She left to work at a school where her beliefs aligned with the school's mission and pedagogical approach, a school that centered students and gave teachers the space and support to be curricularly creative in response to their students. The practice of looking closely at students and their passions stayed at the center of her work and continues to motivate and inspire her curricular design and responsive teaching.

Take creative risks to center student voice

Nia

In her nineteenth year of teaching, Nia felt confident in building classroom community and in her command of whole-class instruction in her fifth-grade classroom. She now wanted to explore her practice around differentiation of instruction. She could tell that most of her students were "doing okay" but worried about "a couple of those who struggle" or who "have short attention, have a hard time focusing." For example, in reviewing Anthony's writing notebook, Nia felt frustrated with the low ratio of reading response sentences written to pictures of cartoons drawn. She felt that Anthony was capable of more expressive extended writing but that he was not engaged with the work and was distracting himself. On the other hand, Jane produced plenty of writing but sat silently through group conversations and whole-class instruction. Nia was concerned that Jane's lack of participation was limiting her learning. These individual needs were not exactly Nia's motivation for change, but they contributed to her feeling that she could reach more of her students on a deeper level. She had been researching integrating multimodal projects and approaches into classroom instruction and was intrigued by how these practices might help her make learning more engaging for and responsive to all of her students. She was apprehensive, however, about how to employ these practices, given the rigid prescriptive curriculum of her school.

In her research into multimodality, Nia had learned about imagery and the power of collage to represent and develop complex ideas. Collage felt like a very approachable kind of project to add to her curriculum. She did not think it would take much time away from other curricular obligations, and it would be easy enough for her students to do without much additional support from her. She decided that she would take a chance and play with her school's curriculum by modifying a written assignment to be a multimodal project. Where originally her school curriculum had assigned a history biography writing unit, Nia decided to have her students complete their biographies of inspirational people from history as collages accompanied by short essays. As she explained:

> When I taught biography the year before, children wrote traditional research papers. And what we found was that they were not invested in the process. This process would allow children to look at pictures, think about words that they would use to describe the person they were learning about, and then make connections with the visuals and with words.

It was a seemingly small shift, but Nia found the impact significant. Her students' essays had more complex, meaningful, and relevant ideas than she had seen in previous years. She also saw that they drew more connections between the subjects of their biographies and themselves. Generally, she observed that her students seemed to be more engaged during classwork time. In particular, Anthony worked hard on this project, producing a beautiful collage and a rich accompanying essay.

Nia was excited about what multimodal instruction might do for her students and decided to push against the prescribed curriculum a little more with the upcoming unit. This unit was meant to be a standardized testing unit wherein students would receive passages to read and answer multiple-choice and short-answer questions based on those readings. Nia knew that the repetitive practice would bore most of her students and alienate others completely, so she decided to take a different approach. In this particular year, Nia had a group of students who regularly brought issues of racial injustice to morning meeting conversations and who expressed interest in and curiosity about activism. She felt that "even though it was test prep time, and even though the civil rights movement was not a part of our curriculum, it was important for students to see how in the past, injustices were done to people and how those people were able to fight back." She wanted to find a way to teach content that her students would connect with, use teaching methods that would be accessible and engaging for all of her students, and do so under the guise of test prep.

Curate accessible and relevant content

Her first step was cultivating a rich text set of readings, speeches, poetry, and videos about or from the civil rights movement. As daily test prep, she would share one of these texts with the class along with a set of multiple-choice and short-response questions to complete. She carefully designed the multiple-choice and short-answer questions to mimic the testing material they would have been using for the mandated test prep unit. Her structure ensured that all of her students were practicing test taking as they would engage with it on the state exams. The varied texts diminished the boredom of daily repetition. They also allowed her to support all of her students in learning test-taking practice, even those who were developing the decoding or comprehension skills to read a fifth-grade-level text. Centering the daily readings around a theme of shared interest gave her students some purpose with this test prep portion of the unit. They were engaging with the texts and even with the test practice for a reason other than to prepare for the state exams, for a reason that they cared about.

Design engaging learning experiences

That purpose was then strengthened by the other portion of the unit that Nia designed. Rather than focusing the unit on the consumption of information and accuracy in test scores, Nia centered the class work on the students' production of their own knowledge. Using student interest surveys, she generated a menu of different ways that her students could work to express their understanding of the civil rights movement and its application to their lives. Her students wanted to create skits, do a poetry study, research and recreate a resistance movement from the past, prepare a video presentation, and write reports on a critical feature of the civil rights movement. The students used Nia's menu of project options to decide which small group they would join. Nia's work was to learn to support them in developing these projects as they collected information from their shared "test prep" readings to design something of their own, representative of their knowledge about the civil rights movement and its connections to their own ideas about activism. During this project development, Nia got to see students like Jane engaging with her peers as they created work together.

How it turned out

In reflecting on her experience, Nia noted that "there are so many demands on how we teach, the methods that we use, what we teach, the curriculum of the day, it often leaves little room for teachers to incorporate what they know is best for children." By restructuring her test prep to center it around content that was engaging for students and through the use of multimodal and multiply accessible means of representing information and expressing their understanding (CAST.org), Nia was able to make more space for what she knew was best for her students.

Nia's administration did not explicitly allow this work. At the beginning of her adapted unit, she chose to close the door and enact the curriculum in private. As the unit moved forward successfully and students were engaged and participatory in both the test prep portion of their work and the development of their projects, Nia felt a little more secure letting other teachers see what she and her students were doing. In her opinion, the risk paid off when, "In the end, students walked away having studied the civil rights movement, knowing more about it than they may have given other learning approaches, and able to make meaningful connections to their lives and the circumstances around them."

While Nia saw the impact on her students, I saw the impact of this creative risk on her as an educator. She was teaching content about which she was passionate. She was being innovative and pushing herself to learn new things like tech skills, which she had been afraid of allowing into the classroom, but that enriched her students' learning experiences. She started with her door closed, a seasoned teacher following a prescriptive curriculum with grace and command of the content, and she became a veteran teacher with her door open, leading the way for the school in building responsive and engaging curriculum that centered students' voices.

Capitalize on resistance, teach a different hidden curriculum
Klaudia

During Klaudia's fourth year as a teacher, she was working as a Special Education Teacher Support Services (SETSS) provider. Her students were an all-male cohort, all of whom spoke Spanish as a primary language and all of whom had been diagnosed with a disability. These young men were placed in general education and Integrated Co-Teaching (ICT) classrooms for high school English but were not completing much of the work in those classes, often not attending classes, and were classified as "frustrating" by most of their teachers. They were placed in Klaudia's class to receive SETSS in order to improve their performance in their English classes and on their high school English state exam. Klaudia's principal gave her a set of English exam test prep books to use as her curriculum for the class.

Recognize student resistance, power, and capacity

Klaudia's students were immediately resistant to the test prep book. Having been subjected to repetitive test prep curricula year after year, they were utterly unwilling to engage with this work again, and Klaudia did not blame them. However, she felt a responsibility to support them in being ready to take the exams that would determine their readiness to graduate from high school. She wondered if it would make sense to leverage their resistance as a starting point to build their engagement (Annamma and Morrison, 2018; Shor, 1996). Her students were right that the test prep book likely would not help them prepare for or pass the state exam, and she engaged in that conversation with them. But that did not mean they were incapable of preparing for and passing that exam, and Klaudia also engaged in that conversation with her students. She challenged them to deconstruct their test prep book and collaboratively build a different tool for preparing for the test. Her process had to start with creating a space for her students to critique the test and the prep book. She got copies of old tests and let them go through these and their prep book, simply sharing their thoughts. Often, when students complain about these things, we as teachers respond with a very unsatisfying, "I know, but if you want to pass the test," dismissal of students' critiques. Klaudia instead took the time to hold class discussions focused on critiquing the tests and working with her students to document their critiques and categorize them.

Through this work, Klaudia and her students realized that they had two lines of work to pursue: 1) creating a study guide or approach that they felt would help them prepare for the exam, and 2) understanding who designed the tests and the test prep and where they should send their analysis and critique. They began by exploring what the exam was supposed to test. Through an analysis of the old tests Klaudia had collected, they determined that the test was supposed to test their reading comprehension, skills with text analysis and the use of evidence, and essay composition, including organization and writing conventions. Her students were astounded to discover the simplicity and breadth of what they were being tested on, given how unengaging and irrelevant the content and the test itself had always felt. This prompted a reinvigorated line of questions about who designed this exam and the test prep for it, but it also empowered them to think of all of the multiple ways that they could study and prepare for the test. Interestingly, as they built their own test prep guide, bringing in materials to study with and designing questions for each other, they did not entirely abandon the test prep book that the principal had assigned them. Instead, they used it as a resource for structure and to evaluate the test prep materials that they were creating.

Simultaneously, Klaudia felt it was important to honor the outrage they had felt and help them find a way to voice their frustrations and dismay at the content of the exam and in the test prep book. She offered her students time and support in pursuing the questions and critiques they had raised in class regarding the exam. She had them do the research and find answers to their own questions. Her students had many critiques to offer in their discussions, but writing was a barrier to their engagement in any strategic movement forward from their critiques. Klaudia taught them about multiple digital tools they could use to capture their thinking and had them design other ways to present their findings. Her students "were so good at it that they started to learn how to do things that I didn't know how to do." Klaudia also told her students that they needed to determine to whom they should send their analysis and critiques if they wanted to be heard. Her students responded well to this approach; rather than being bored, dismissive, or disengaged, they were now "working on something that matters now because we are the ones who asked these questions."

How it turned out

The relevance of their work was apparent to her students, but because this was a Special education support class, they were not receiving school credit for their work. Her students had expressed frustration over this, so Klaudia reached out to the general education English teacher who taught most of her students English. She wanted to work with the teacher to find a way for her students to receive school credit in their English course for the work that they were completing in her class. Klaudia collaborated with the English teacher to provide credit for her students' digital representations that included embedded text. This additional motivation pushed many of Klaudia's students to write short essays describing the concepts they had already communicated digitally.

What is more, Klaudia's collaboration with the English teacher stretched the curricular change she had implemented in her own classroom into the general education classroom. Klaudia saw the power of her work as it began to spread to other classrooms through her students. She knew that she had allowed her students to push back. She knew that by pursuing the line of critical questioning, she was teaching a different hidden curriculum, one to speak back to the hidden curriculum of the school that wanted them to be compliant and complacent. This strategic creativity continued to inspire Klaudia in her SETSS classroom and began to filter into other modes of her work. She started writing IEPs for her students from this perspective, enriched with creativity and resistance to underlying exclusionary schooling standards. The more of this subversive work she did, the better her students performed and the more her administration wanted to support her efforts, to the point where they sponsored her to pursue an additional degree at an elite school of education in their city.

Be a creative intellectual, not a technocratic robot

If you are reading any of this and feeling excited about curricular re/design, you are in luck, my friend. Resources abound, and Google is your friend. Brilliant teachers and scholars across many years and in multiple countries have designed and shared curricula, design frameworks, curricular design tools, educational technology, thinking routines – the list goes on – that you can use to get creative in your local context with your students. I will share a list of some of my favorite tools at the end of this chapter, but if curricular design were the heart of the issue, it would not have a place in this book. Unfortunately, the heart of the issue is the growing lack of space, time, expectation, or freedom for teachers to play with the curriculum they teach in creative and responsive ways. Curriculum may be "the centerpiece of educational activity," but what if that curriculum is disengaging, irrelevant, oppressive, or inaccessible to your students? In every course I teach about designing curriculum that is accessible and culturally responsive (Waitoller and King-Thorius, 2016), my students are excited about the possibility of actually reaching their students and just as overwhelmed about how they will be able to do any of that work given the curricular restraints of their schools. What I would like to offer you to consider is not the *what* of the curricular play that Luz, Nia, and Klaudia engaged in, but rather the *why*, the *how*, and the *why again*.

Why curricular play

Being curricularly responsive to your students *is* social justice and inclusivity. Even when working from a social justice-oriented prescribed curriculum, teachers are still uniquely positioned to be the ones re/designing inclusive and responsive learning experiences for their students because they interact daily with their particular students (Trinter and Hughes, 2021). Audit culture-driven policy reforms, however, do not trust teachers to be decision-makers or intellectuals (Taubman, 2010). Instead, they position teachers as agents of social control whose work is to "maintain the status quo instead of attempting to transform the world through their work" (Aydarova, 2021, p. 682). The prescribed curriculum that leaves you no room to be responsive to your students, that positions you as a technocratic disseminator of standardized information, is an intentional tool to prevent teachers from being agents of social change. To be an agent of change, to teach for social justice and inclusivity, you must at the very least question the curriculum you are required to teach and then, like Luz, Nia, and Klaudia, find even small ways to act if you believe that curricular requirements are harming or limiting your students.

How to bring about responsive curricular change

Teaching for social justice and inclusivity is a passion and a commitment, but teaching is also a job, and I am not advocating for you to risk your livelihood by dismissing the requirements of your position. None of the educators in this chapter dismissed their job requirements, even as they subversively acted to change the curriculum in their classrooms. They did, however, make strategic choices in order to disrupt the status quo. Luz, for example, collected as much data as she could to support her decisions because she understood the power of "data" in an audit culture. She also intentionally centered her work around students with IEPs because of the weight that legal obligations could lend to her decisions. While her decision-making might be easily questioned and diminished in her technocratic context, she could borrow legitimacy from the system's sanctioned power sources.

Nia started so small with her subversive curricular moves that they were almost imperceptible to her colleagues and administration; they were just lovely arts add-ons to a standard unit. When she shared the student outcomes from her work and received enthusiastic encouragement from her administration, she felt more confident in making more significant changes. Even as she moved to make those more significant changes, she was 1) careful to maintain the administrative curricular requirements around test preparation and 2) careful about when to invite her administration witness the student outcomes. Nia borrowed legitimacy for her decision-making from the test scores and student outcomes that ruled her context. Klaudia kept the curricular requirements of her classroom intact, but rather than moving through the prescriptive curriculum and robotically communicating an oppressive hidden curriculum, she taught a different hidden curriculum about resistance and advocacy. She did not need to legitimize her choices because she was using the prescribed curriculum. To the extent that she did so, she was able to demonstrate student task completion, another marker of success in an audit culture.

Teacher resilience through curricular play

Being curricularly responsive to your students is social justice and inclusivity. I know I wrote that above, but I am restating it here to speak to you and your resilience as an educator, more so than about your students and what they deserve. If you are working in the field of education as a teacher committed to social justice and inclusivity, and if day in and day out you are teaching someone else's teaching points, dragging your students through the lessons, wondering what they are even learning, you will burn out. Curricular design and even small curricular play can be challenging work to engage in, intellectually and professionally. However, it can also be some of the most rewarding work you can do as a teacher for social justice and inclusivity. As Luz, Nia, and Klaudia all demonstrate, a primary reward of curricular design and play is student engagement and learning. Each of them was able to experience the reward of designing something that worked for their students, which is an ultimately satisfying feeling for an educator.

Farris-Berg and Dirkswager (2012) propose that the autonomy to be a creative decision-maker can foster ownership for teachers, buy-in to the school community, and, subsequently resilience. When educators have opportunities to experiment with new teaching methods, design innovative lessons, or incorporate student choice in projects, they cultivate problem-solving skills that equip them to tackle classroom challenges with a sense of agency (McKimmie et al., 2019). Moreover, the act of being creative itself can act as a stress buffer, allowing teachers to tap into a sense of playfulness and flow (Sawyer, 2011). Creative play has been shown to reduce burnout and reignite the passion for teaching, fostering motivation and perseverance (McKimmie et al., 2019).

Finally, for teachers committed to social justice and inclusivity, this curricular play is an act of resistance, and there is something powerful and seductive in knowing that you are acting to resist, acting to make change (Schlessinger, 2018). The act of resistance, in and of itself, can support your resilience, as you can consciously own that you are not perpetuating the status quo and that you are being the agent of change you set out to be.

Developing practices for curricular play that foster resilience

Who designed the curriculum that you have been asked to teach? What was motivating them? What does your school's curricular approach message about its students? About its teachers? If you think you might be ready to build your resilience through curricular play, these resources may be a place to start.

1. **Start with Curricular Analysis:** It is important to work from a point of knowledge and understanding. Make sure you understand the standards and content your current curriculum is teaching and the structure of its design. This will allow you to be strategic in your choices for what to hold on to in order to work within administrative requirements and what you can play with in the content or the instructional design.

2. **Data is King:** Document everything you do. Document your student's learning, their behaviors, their feedback. Start documenting before you change anything, and do not ever stop. Your data will be your power.

3. **Make Small Moves and Share Victories:** Curricular design can be really complex and overwhelming, especially at first. Making transgressive moves in your job can be terrifying. Start small to test your limits and those of your administration. Grow your practice as you better understand where you will have space to play. And with every small change you make, share the victories. This will provide a foundation for your administration to trust your decision-making.

4. **Teach Your Own Hidden Curriculum:** Sometimes, we cannot change the content we are teaching, but we can

teach other perspectives or even critiques of the content. Teaching your students to be critical readers of their world and their schooling can be just as powerful as teaching them content that they connect to.

5. **Let Yourself Out of the Box:** Creativity and intellectual play are good for you. There is no reason why every lesson needs to follow an "I do, we do, you do" direct instruction structure. There is no reason why students' understanding must or even should be measured by tests or essays. Give your creative muscles some exercise and try something different. Check out that World Wide Web for inspiration.

6. **Seriously, Get on the Internet:** Teachers are doing really cool things in their classrooms. Education scholars have developed really helpful frameworks and tools to support the education of critical and thoughtful students. You do not have to start from scratch; you do not have to reinvent the wheel.

Curricular play curricular extension

Start with Curricular Analysis: Make sure you understand the standards, content, and methods your current curriculum is teaching and the structure of its design. This will allow you to be strategic in your choices for what to hold on to in order to work within administrative requirements and what you can play with in the content or the instructional design.

1) Take the curriculum you have been asked to teach and begin to analyze it by retrofitting that curriculum into the Wiggins and McTighe (2006) Understanding By Design Template (2.0). For more support in understanding this template, check out this white paper on Understanding by Design (McTighe and Wiggins, 2012).

2) Once you have deconstructed your prescribed or assigned curriculum, annotate it to consider where you might play to make it more accessible? More responsive? More engaging?

Stage 1 Desired Results		
ESTABLISHED GOALS <type here>	*Transfer*	
	Students will be able to independently use their learning to… <type here>	
	Meaning	
	UNDERSTANDINGS *Students will understand that…* <type here>	ESSENTIAL QUESTIONS <type here>
	Acquisition	
	Students will know… <type here>	Students will be skilled at… <type here>
Stage 2 – Evidence		
Evaluative Criteria	**Assessment Evidence**	
<type here>	PERFORMANCE TASK(S): <type here>	
<type here>	OTHER EVIDENCE: <type here>	
Stage 3 – Learning Plan		
Summary of Key Learning Events and Instruction <type here>		

5
Loving learning communities

In the last few chapters, I have argued that acting within your classroom practice to teach for social justice and inclusivity can, in and of itself, be a way to build your resilience as an agent of educational change within restrictive, oppressive, and exclusionary contexts. While that holds, enacting these practices also requires a bit of bravery and confidence, which can be hard to come by on your own. There are two out-of-classroom practices that are instrumental to enacting the previous in-classroom practices and building teacher resilience: finding community and pursuing professional growth. In each of the preceding chapters, I have made reference to the colleagues, mentors, and professional development opportunities that Catherine, Grace, Luz, Nia, and Klaudia relied on and were inspired by as they reflected on their commitments and practices. This chapter explores how investing in a community of like-minded peers and in one's own education inspires and sustains educators who are teaching for social justice and inclusivity.

You need your people

I met Daniel and Shota and they met each other in their teacher residency program. They both identified as straight cis men of color, and they were both pursuing certifications in special education. In a teaching force that was approximately 80 percent white, with 75 percent of all special educators identifying as women, Daniel and Shota were both clear outliers. This was true in their graduate program and even more so when they entered the field full-time. In each of their separate schools, they stood out as "the only" in one respect or another. They also carried with them all of the weight and responsibility of being men in schools, and specifically of being men of color in schools. Because of their social identities, they were positioned as disciplinarians, asked to take on complicated issues with students simply because they "could relate to them better," and were underestimated as intellectuals and educators. These microaggressions from their students, their students' caregivers, their colleagues, and their administrations were not unexpected (Daftary et al., 2024), but they were constant and beyond frustrating.

The isolation and dehumanization that Daniel and Shota experienced because of their gender and race were only exacerbated by their deep and meaningful commitments to social justice and inclusivity. They had studied Critical Race Theory (CRT) and disability studies in education (DSE). They had learned about and were building their practices of Universal Design for Learning and Culturally Responsive Pedagogy (see previous chapters) in their curricular design and enactment. They were building relationships with their students, and they were practicing pedagogies of love in their classrooms and through their extracurricular clubs and athletic coaching. As they did this work that they believed in and had been taught to do and to prioritize through their social justice-driven inclusive education graduate school program, they felt more and more ostracized by their colleagues.

Shota

At regular Friday happy hours, Shota would hear his coworkers complain about their shared students and refer to some of his male students of color as "lazy" or "resistant." Labeling students of color as "lazy" reinforces negative stereotypes that have long existed within the educational system. These stereotypes erroneously imply that students of color are less intelligent or lack motivation rather than recognize the systemic oppression of people of color in US schooling. Similarly, "resistant" implies that the problem lies in the student's unwillingness to cooperate with the dominant culture of the school rather than in the dominant and oppressive culture of the school itself (Ferguson, 2020). Shota knew that the way we talk about our students matters. He knew that even if unwittingly, these words carried an implied negativity and deficit perspective about his students and maybe even about him. He had lived that experience, he had studied the mechanisms of racism and ableism driving a school system grounded in white supremacy, and he was committed to teaching for social justice and inclusivity through anti-racist and anti-ableist pedagogies. When he heard his coworkers disparaging his students in the casual context of a teacher happy hour, he felt helpless. He was unsure how to act or speak up to disrupt these problematic characterizations. He was miserable at the thought of not standing up at all to disrupt these problematic characterizations of his students, and he was wholly unsure how to move forward with his professional relationships with his colleagues. As a result, he felt himself pulling back more and more from his colleagues, skipping happy hours, and spending all of his time at school with his students, the people to whom he did feel a connection. While those relationships with his students were rewarding, Shota felt the absence of a community of peers to engage with. He had no one to problem-solve with him around curriculum or student support. He had no one to talk to and commiserate with about the intensity of being a teacher. He felt lonely, and it made the work even harder.

Daniel

At the same time, a bridge and a borough away, Daniel was encountering his own conflict that had him feeling underestimated as an educator. Daniel was working in a school with a shifting and gentrifying population. While the school had traditionally served Black and Brown students from households operating under the poverty line, over the past few years, with neighborhood changes, there were more and more white students from affluent households joining the school community. These two populations of students had, generally speaking, different educational opportunities and lived experiences. Daniel was working to build community and curriculum that bridged these divides, that attended to the skills and needs of all the students in his classroom, and that supported them in learning from each other. As a relatively new teacher, this was quite the challenge, but it motivated Daniel. He saw the need for and the complexity of a responsive history curriculum that spoke to and engaged all of his students. He was exploring methods to support students who encountered reading or writing barriers to be full participants in the classroom work in rigorous ways.

However, in this work, Daniel encountered a barrier of his own. A parent of one of his students began to insert herself into his practices. She would find him after school or at the weekend chess matches he chaperoned for his students and ask him about his assignments. She would bring her son's work with her and show Daniel where he had not graded it "correctly." Daniel had no problem with feedback or with being pushed in his thinking in general, but this was something different. This parent was asserting her perspective and desires in a way that undercut him and devalued the social justice orientation and inclusivity of his work. What is more, he noticed that this parent was not assertive in this way with other teachers who taught her child. While he had perfectly amiable relationships with those teachers, they did not seem to value or take seriously his perspective on his curriculum and the conflict with this parent. When he went to his administration to seek support, he was met with empty words and inaction.

Daniel and Shota: Have your people

Fortunately, Daniel and Shota had each other. When they felt ostracized and devalued for the social justice-oriented, inclusive work that they were attempting to do in their schools, when they felt stereotyped or dehumanized because of the intersection of their race and gender, they would reach out to each other. They would vent, ask for advice or help to solve a problem, or just provide each other with a little compassion and empathy. Over time, it became clear to them that they were each other's support system and most significant colleague, even though they did not work at the same school. They would meet for their own happy hour, which they eventually transformed into a non-alcohol-driven hangout in order to prioritize their mental wellness. When Shota was frustrated with his students and needed to vent, he could text Daniel and have someone who would listen to him without making racist or ableist assumptions about his students. When Daniel had to manage the complex tensions arising from his administration's attempts to assuage some of the more aggressive parents in the community, he had Shota to help him think through his own curricular moves and problem-solve.

Daniel and Shota plus: Grow your people

The teacher residency cohort Daniel and Shota had been part of was made up of a group of preservice teachers who had really cared for each other, emotionally and intellectually. One of my colleagues and I had hosted the cohort for monthly meetups as part of a research project that we were working on and, frankly, because we really liked them and did not want to lose them after graduation. We structured these meetups around big ideas that we thought our former students might be grappling with, given the tensions between their graduate school learning and the realities of schooling. Daniel and Shota used these spaces as another point of connection with each other and also found more community. They leaned on their cohort to process the tensions that they were experiencing, to speak explicitly and clearly about structural racism and ableism within their schools, and to be affirmed in their experiences, their thinking, and their classroom enactments. In these spaces, where they were with *their* community, they could argue, disagree, and come away feeling loved AND with new ideas for their classrooms and schools.

How it turned out

Having each other and having their grad school cohort did not fix the problematic contexts of their schools. They both ended up leaving those first schools and finding new jobs but with empowering support from each other. Rather than turning away from education altogether, Daniel and Shota helped each other hold on to their passion to teach for social justice and inclusivity. They helped each other identify that it was not the teaching or the students pushing them out but rather the school communities that they were attempting to operate within. They helped each other think through what they could endure from the faculty of a school they were going to work in, given that they anticipated encountering oppressive structures of schooling anywhere they went. This support of each other helped them find their different but sustainable paths forward at new schools, where they both had an easier time finding "their people" within the school community. The connection they built with each other during that residency year was instrumental in their resilience and eventual longevity in the field. Daniel and Shota used their shared experiences of exclusion and their shared commitments to social justice and inclusivity to build a deep and meaningful friendship. They stood up at each other's weddings. They watched as their families grew. They coached each other through career changes. They shared friendship, they shared teaching, they shared teaching for social justice and inclusivity, and they shared love for each other.

Elevate yourself, elevate the profession

The final narrative of this text does not focus on a person but rather on a group of people and a professional development vision and project. As part of a citywide special education reform effort, the Teachers College Inclusive Classroom Project (TCICP) was invited by the New York City Department of Education to create a "tool kit" for teachers to learn "best practices" to support the inclusion of students with disabilities in general education classrooms. Long weary of watching the integration of students with disabilities into general education classrooms that did not flex to meet the varied needs of a wide range of learners, the TCICP team insisted on a different approach. They knew that teaching inclusively was complicated work, resistant to easy fixes or one-size-fits-all solutions, and they believed in the creative and intellectual capacities of teachers committed to problem-solving for their own classrooms. Accordingly, they designed a professional development opportunity that was driven by individual inquiry explored in collaboration with like-minded educators in communities of study (Ainscow and Sandill, 2010; Naraian, 2016).

Teams of 10–30 teachers and one project facilitator met monthly throughout the school year to learn and explore the complexities of a particular practice for inclusivity:

- Collaboration and co-planning among teachers;
- Designing accessible curricula;

- Integrating technology in the classroom;
- Building restorative justice practices; and
- Working with communities and families.

In these monthly sessions, the inquiry teams worked together to consider their specific practice and how it could be used to teach all students and build a responsive and inclusive environment. As the year progressed, the participants would bring dilemmas from their classrooms and schools related to their inquiry team's focal practice. They were provided with concepts, strategies, and research to support their work in their chosen focal area. Team members:

1. Planned, enacted, and collected data to understand the impact of their teaching moves;
2. Developed professional development sessions and facilitated these sessions at an annual citywide conference for their peers; and
3. Published their work on the organization's website as part of a collection honoring teacher's practices.

I worked for TCICP for six years, first as a sort of teaching assistant for the inquiry team facilitators, then as a research assistant for the project, and along the way as a facilitator of inquiry teams. In this capacity, I had the opportunity to participate in teams, observe team meetings, and follow teachers into their schools to see their enactments. Through my involvement, I met and worked with university-based professors, leading educational consultants, principals and district leaders, and teachers from grades K–12 across all general education content areas and in all special education positions. All of these people, across all of their various positions in schools and in the hierarchy of schooling, were members of the inquiry team. Every member of the team had chosen to be there. Every member of the team was invested in building a more inclusive classroom, school, or even district. And so, every member of every team was there to learn and to support each other.

As I have mentioned in previous chapters, teachers are often conceived of in ways that deintellectualize their work or deskill it. Scripted curricula are put in place to ensure that schooling is "teacher proof" to protect our students from bad teachers. The assumption that teachers are the problem ignores all of the structures that devalue teaching as a profession: low pay, top-down decision-making, hyper accountability, and a continued devolution of teacher preparation programs. Low pay, lack of respect, and demanding workloads contribute to teacher shortages, particularly in underserved schools. Fewer qualified teachers leads to a decline in educational quality, further discouraging potential educators. While audit culture, top-down decision-making, and strict adherence to disciplinary procedures and scripted lessons can work to deintellectualize and deskill teachers, fostering teacher autonomy and supporting teachers' professional development can have the opposite impact.

Teachers as intellectual, skilled, and autonomous professionals

What happened at TCICP was just this. At the beginning of every inquiry cycle – a late September or early October start – the rooms at the university would fill up with an evidently trepidatious group of educators and an even more evidently anxious team facilitator, the so-called "expert" in the field. The school-based teachers in the room were very used to traditional professional development experiences: a day or two sitting and being told "best practices" that they should implement and how to do so. They were looking to the inquiry facilitator to give them some good "takeaways" that they could "turnkey" for their schools, and they were not clear on why they needed to come back month after month for this. The facilitators, on the other hand, were used to similar structures of professional development or to university teaching and were wary of what was going to happen when they asked a group of full-time educators – whom they were not grading and who did not work for them – to engage in deep and scholarly action research over the course of an entire school year. But by the end of that first session, without exception, the air was electric with possibility.

During the six hours of that first session, a few things became clear to everyone in the room. First, there was not a singular expert. There were shared commitments to social justice and inclusivity and a shared curiosity about *co-planning*, or *accessible curriculum design*, or *restorative justice*. And there were the resources that each person in that room brought, be it from the research they had conducted and published, the class that they had taught the day before, or their own experiences as students. Second, there was nothing to "turnkey," and no "best practice" was being sold. The day had been spent reading, thinking, and talking about social justice, inclusivity, and the focal practice of the team, and there was no solution presented. Instead, there was an invitation from TCICP to be a teacher-researcher as part of a team and supported by the professional development project. I remember one inquiry team participant recounting her experience of that day as simultaneously invigorating and annoying. "I didn't know what to expect, I didn't know what inquiry really meant or what they wanted from me, but I knew I was excited."

Not everyone came back the following month, but those who did, came back with observations from their classrooms and schools and ready to dig into the work. Through their work as inquiry team members, they began to see themselves differently. They had come to professional development expecting to be receptacles and conduits for other people's ideas, but through their collective work, they became producers of their own knowledge and practices. They read research to help them develop ideas. They unpacked their questions to get to the heart of their concerns and push through the murkiness of structural racism, institutionalized ableism, testing, and accountability that clouded their purpose. They analyzed data from their classrooms with their colleagues. Eventually, they brought the practices and professional development to their schools, but as their own, fully backed by research in the field and their own research in their classroom contexts. When they got pushback from their administration or colleagues, resistance to the changes that schools need to make to be more social justice-oriented and inclusive, they had answers from their research and a built-in community of like-minded professionals to turn to for support. When they published their work through conference presentations and website contributions, they added a line to their résumés and recognized their own contributions to the field.

Elevate yourself

TCICP professional development offered its participants an opportunity to see their competency and enact their commitments. Teaching is presented to us and understood societally as this technocratic act of guiding students through a prescribed curriculum. The more we engage in that trope, the less empowered we feel to do the critically responsive work of teaching for social justice and inclusivity. Professional development (PD) almost always means attending someone else's workshop about how you should be doing your job. To be clear, I do not intend to disparage those PD opportunities. There are a lot of really excellent PD opportunities out there designed in just this way to teach educators a specific approach or strategy to use in their classroom. That said, my intention here is to elevate the idea that you, the reader of this text, are a creative, critical, intellectual problem-solver whose work is complex. Teaching for social justice and inclusivity can be lonely and isolating work that makes you question yourself and your competency. TCICP offered the inquiry members an opportunity to rewrite that narrative, to position themselves as knowers, and as part of the larger conversation on educational equity.

Seeing yourself as a contributing voice rather than a conduit for other people's ideas requires us to engage in three significant practices of the academic space: knowing the research in the field, articulating our own work as part of the field, and sharing our work with the field. Knowing the research in the field opens us up to new and sometimes inspiring ideas. This was evident, for example, for members of the *multimodal inquiry team*, many of whom had never even heard the term "multimodal" before, let alone integrated it into their teaching practice. Knowing the scholarship helps us be thoughtfully critical of practices that seem problematic in our schools. This was the case for a few members of the *restorative justice inquiry team* who quickly realized that what their schools were calling restorative justice was not working because it, in fact, was not restorative justice. Knowing the research allows us to speak with an authority that, unfortunately, our classroom expertise does not always instill in our colleagues and administration, like when the members of the *co-teaching and co-planning inquiry team* insisted that special education teachers should be working with their general education counterparts to plan lessons and not retroactively modifying already planned lessons.

Knowing the research and scholarship in the field also sets the stage for teachers to own their work in meaningful ways that honor its complexity. Across my years in schools, I have heard too many incredible teachers speak about their brilliant, responsive work in their classrooms as "just" this or that practice. I will reiterate here that teaching is not easy, especially when you are teaching for social justice and inclusivity in underserved communities across the diverse needs of our changing societal landscape. It is never "just" anything. When you know the research in the field, you can see and name the complexity of your work as part of the larger conversation on educational equity. This was clear when the *literacy supports inquiry team* analyzed their classroom instruction as a combination of Universal Design for Learning and Culturally Relevant Pedagogy components to teach reading in engaging, accessible, and responsive ways. So much scholarly work in the field of education, mine included, comes from the practices of teachers; teachers should feel empowered to and empowered by naming their work as integral to the larger conversation.

To the point of empowerment, sharing your work substantiates that you are, in fact, a part of that larger conversation. That might mean facilitating a school-based PD as many inquiry team members did, presenting at a conference, creating web content, or publishing in books or journals. Inquiry team members did all of these things. For some, the achievement and the sharing of their work at the end of the inquiry year was a culminating highlight as TCICP had designed it. For others, that presentation of their learning was when they understood that they had something to contribute beyond their classroom and that there were platforms to do that. Sharing their work inspired them to do more, seek out more learning opportunities (so many went back to school), start new initiatives, or move into leadership positions in their schools. Being part of TCICP inquiry teams elevated members in their careers and elevated the profession by demonstrating how much teachers know and have to contribute to the field. That energy, that sense of worth and value, builds teacher resilience.

Learning in loving community

TCICP's other significant offering was the people who came together to do this work. University-based professors; leading educational consultants; principals and district leaders; teachers from grades K–12 across all general education content areas and in all special education positions; doctoral students trying to understand what they were doing in higher education … we all came together to learn together and to learn from each other. The structure of these spaces, the pedagogies of love that came from humans facilitating the teams, not only positioned inquiry team members to see themselves as fully capable, contributing scholars but also offered them space to feel loved, supported, and seen.

TCICP inquiry teams created a space outside of schooling contexts where educators teaching for social justice and inclusivity could feel supported in their ideas, commitments, and disruptive teaching moves. For so many people, these were spaces where educators found the like-mindedness they were looking for and care and support from their teams. When things felt completely dire in the cold, long months of early spring, when it felt like all of the work was amounting to very little change, teams engaged in an exploration of Ellen Moir's (2016) "attitude toward teaching" curve and how that roller coaster of emotion applied to them and their experience. They shared their roadblocks and failures with each other. They listened to each other, sat through tears, and helped each other be in the struggle or find ways to move forward.

When an inquiry member was losing track of the social justice aims of the work or was enacting a practice in a way that would never improve the inclusivity of their classroom, inquiry team members lovingly checked their team members and pushed back against the process. They knew that they had shared goals and that keeping your eye on those goals while navigating the structural racism and institutionalized ableism of schools can be overwhelming. They knew that they had love and support from the members of these teams. That knowledge and foundation allowed them respectfully to disagree with each other and push each other to do their best work. These were collaborative communities built on love, shared commitment, and intellectual participation. They were inspiring, sustaining, and supported their members' autonomy within their individual schools and resilience in their careers.

Developing loving learning communities for resilience

> We are social beings, and we need each other to thrive. A strong, healthy community can bolster us through challenging moments and bring joy to our lives. When we build community, we can build empathy for each other; and building empathy for each other helps us build community.
>
> – Aguilar (2018, p. 95)

I am, by far, not the first person to advocate for teachers to develop strong communities to support them through their careers. In this final chapter, I want to highlight some of the key components I have found to be crucial for developing specifically educational communities that support your resilience as an educator working for social justice and inclusivity. When it comes to building loving relationships and communities centered on social justice and inclusive education, these are my thoughts:

1. **Find your people:** Teaching for social justice and inclusivity can feel isolating. It is work that will burn you out if you do not find your people and invest in the relationships with the folks who make you feel seen and appreciate your perspective.

2. **Affinity groups**: Consider what affinity groups *you* need. Daniel and Shota found each other and saved each other from dehumanization and isolation. It took me way too long to know that talking to other Queer teachers would be instrumental in deepening the love, trust, and vulnerability I could build in my teaching practice. Where will you need support specifically related to your identity? Specifically related to your beliefs? When you see that person in your graduate class or a staff meeting, when you hear them share something that you connect with, invite them out for coffee. You need that person.

3. **Grow affinity groups:** Daniel and Shota had each other, but they also had their larger cohort to contextualize and affirm their experiences. Be open to the idea that there are multiple ways to build affinity, share similar experiences, and learn from differences.

4. **Find the professional development that's "just right" for you**: There are so many communities of educators out there. If you want to learn more about restorative justice, do not just buy a book about it; find the community-based organizations near you that are doing the work already. Find the national institutes that speak to you. As you do, consider how you want to be positioned in professional development. Sometimes, I like to sit and learn about new ideas or practices. More often than not, I find that teachers want to be able to workshop ideas, troubleshoot practices, and make things applicable to their own classroom. Find the professional development opportunities that speak to you and allow you to produce your own knowledge.

5. **Join a "Critical Friends Group"**: Not all Critical Friends Groups are equal, but these can be spaces to build

meaningful relationships with colleagues in and out of your schools and to do deep and critical work around classroom dilemmas and practices.

6. **Know Your Scholars:** When Bettina Love writes a new book, I buy it. When Kylene Beers publishes a revision of her work, I buy it. I follow the people whose work I love on social media. I listen to the podcasts that host my educational heroes. Find the people whose work excites you and make them part of your knowledge and practice. You will be inspired, you will improve your practice, you will be able to speak with the authority not granted to you through your position as a teacher, and you will build your resilience.

7. **Share Your Work:** Find practitioner journals in your content area. Submit to *Rethinking Schools*. See if your graduating institution has a university-hosted blog. Go to education conferences in your field, notice that you can do what the presenter just did, and submit a proposal for the next one. If you need help preparing or submitting a proposal, reach out to your community.

You are not alone in this

I have left you with a lot of suggestions for ways you can build your resilience through reflective work, practices in your classroom, and community with like-minded educators. I do not want you to do this work alone. Know that you are not working alone, even if it sometimes feels that way. There are teachers like you all over the country, working for similar ideals against their versions of the same obstacles. My work, alongside you, is to build teacher education that supports you in this work, teacher education that supports you in being a resilient educator committed to social justice and inclusivity. Maybe, someday, there will be enough of us resilient, responsive, caring, and creative educators out there that we will not have to be so brave or resilient to do what we know is right for our students. You are not alone; others are in this with you, and I am in this with you.

Loving learning communities curricular extension

Finding and investing in your people: Teaching for social justice and inclusivity can feel isolating. It is work that will burn you out if you do not find your people and invest in the relationships with the folks who make you feel seen and appreciate your perspective.

> **Goal:** Your goal is to open up a collaborative and supportive relationship with this person. This relationship could lead to future project collaborations, mentorship opportunities, or simply a valuable connection.
>
> 1) Think about the people you work with right now. Think about your classmates and professors from school. Think about teachers who have inspired you along the way. Can you think of a project you would like to work on with one of them? A conversation that would be inspiring? A problem you could use their help in solving?
> 2) Pick a person you want to reach out to.
> 3) Based on your comfort, draft a letter, email, or scripted conversation to open up a conversation with this person.

Before you write: Here are some questions to consider:
- What are this person's interests and areas of expertise?
- What do I admire about them or want to connect with them about?
- What is the basis of our existing relationship?
- What specific value could I potentially bring to them?
- What kind of support or collaboration am I hoping for?
- What is the overall tone I want to convey?

References

Aguilar, E. (2018). *Onward: Cultivating Emotional Resilience in Educators*. John Wiley & Sons.

Ainscow, M., and Sandill, A. (2010). Developing Inclusive Education Systems: The Role of Organisational Cultures and Leadership. *International Journal of Inclusive Education,* 14(4), pp. 401–416.

American Psychological Association. (2017). *Report of the APA Task Force on Race and the Psychological Profession*. Available at: www.apa.org/about/policy/resolution-combat-racism.pdf [Accessed 8/26/24]

Annamma, S., and Morrison, D. (2018). DisCrit Classroom Ecology: Using Praxis to Dismantle Dysfunctional Education Ecologies. *Teaching and Teacher Education,* 73, pp. 70–80.

Annamma, S. A., Connor, D., and Ferri, B. (2013). Dis/ability Critical Race Studies (DisCrit): Theorizing at the Intersections of Race and Dis/ability. *Race Ethnicity and Education,* 16(1), pp. 1–31.

Apple, M. W. (1976). Making Curriculum Problematic. *The Review of Education / Pedagogy / Cultural Studies,* 2(1), pp. 52–68.

Apple, M. W. (2000). Can Critical Pedagogies Interrupt Rightist Policies? *Educational Theory,* 50(2). 10.1111/j.1741-5446.2000.00229.x.

Artiles, A. J., Trent, S. C., and Palmer, J. (2004). Culturally diverse students in special education: Legacies and prospects. In: J. A. Banks and C. M. Banks, eds., *Handbook of Research on Multicultural Education*. 2nd ed. Jossey-Bass, pp. 716–735.

Artiles, A. I. (2010). From theory to practice in critical disability studies in education. In: L. M. Malti and S. L. Turner, eds., *Disability Studies and the Teachers of Color Project*. Palgrave Macmillan, pp. 139–154.

Artiles, A. J. (2019). Fourteenth Annual Brown Lecture in Education Research: Reenvisioning Equity Research: Disability Identification Disparities as a Case in Point. *Educational Researcher,* 48(6), pp. 325–335. Available at: https://doi.org/10.3102/0013189X19871949 [Accessed 8/26/24].

Asera, R. F. (2016). Culturally biased testing in a standards-based era. *Educational Researcher, 45*(8), pp. 482–491.

Ashby, C. (2012). Disability Studies and Inclusive Teacher Preparation: A Socially Just Path for Teacher Education. *Research and Practice for Persons with Severe Disabilities,* 37(2), pp. 89–99.

Aydarova, E. (2021). Building a One-Dimensional Teacher: Technocratic Transformations in Teacher Education Policy Discourses. *Educational Studies,* 57(6), pp. 670–689. Available at: https://doi.org/10.1080/00131946.2021.1969934 [Accessed 8/26/24]

Bailey, T. (Host), and Oyler, C. (2024, April 1). *Teacher preparation for today's schools.* [audio podcast]. Pursuing the public good. Teachers College, Columbia University. Available at: https://www.tc.columbia.edu/digitalfuturesinstitute/media/pursuing-the-public-good/teacher-preparation-for-todays-schools/ [Accessed 8/26/24]

Biklen, D., and Burke, J. (2006). Presuming competence. *Equity & Excellence in Education,* 39(2), pp. 166–175.

Broderick, A. A., and Leonardo, Z. (2016). What a good boy. In: D. J. Connor, B. A. Ferri, and S. A. Annamma, eds., *DisCrit: Disability Studies and Critical Race Theory in Education.* New York: Teachers College Press, pp. 55–67.

CAST. (n.d.). Universal Design for Learning Center. Available at: https://www.cast.org/ [Accessed 8/26/24]

Castro, A.J., Kelly, J. and Shih, M. (2018), *Resilience strategies for new teachers in high-needs areas*, Teaching and Teacher Education, Vol. 26 No.3, pp.622–629.

Connor, D., Ferri, B., and Annamma, S. A. eds. (2016). *DisCrit: Disability Studies and Critical Race Theory in Education*. New York: Teachers College Press.

Daftary, A. M. H., Ortega, D., Samimi, C., and Ball, A. (2024). "Did I Hear That Right?": A CRT Analysis of Racial Microaggressions in K–12 Schools. *Affilia*, 39(2), pp. 285–301.

Dei, G. J. S., and McDermott, M., eds. (2014). Introduction to *The Politics of Anti-Racism Education: In Search of Strategies for Transformative Learning*. Springer Netherlands, pp. 1–11.

Delgado, R., and Stefancic, J. (2023). *Critical Race Theory: An Introduction*. 4th ed. New York: NYU Press.

Deliovsky, K. (2010). *White Femininity: Race, Gender & Power*. Fernwood.

Drew, S. V., and Sosnowski, C. (2019). Emerging Theory of Teacher Resilience: A Situational Analysis. *English Teaching: Practice & Critique*, 18(4), pp. 492–507.

Farris-Berg, K., and Dirkswager, E. J. (2012). *Trusting Teachers with School Success: What Happens When Teachers Call the Shots*. R&L Education.

Ferguson, A. A. (2020). *Bad Boys: Public Schools in the Making of Black Masculinity*. Ann Arbor: University of Michigan Press.

Ferguson, P. M., and Nusbaum, E. (2012). Disability Studies: What Is It and What Difference Does It Make? *Research and Practice for Persons with Severe Disabilities*, 37(2), pp. 70–80.

Fredricks, J. A., Hofkens, T., and Belongie, C. (2019). The Causal Effects of Student Engagement on Academic Performance: A Systematic Review. *International Journal of Education Research*, 90, pp. 174–194.

Garland-Thomson, R. (2017). *Extraordinary Bodies: Figuring Physical Disability in American Culture and Literature*. New York: Columbia University Press.

Gay, G. (2010). Acting on Beliefs in Teacher Education for Cultural Diversity. *Journal of Teacher Education,* 61(1–2), pp. 143–152.

Giroux, H. A. (2010). Rethinking Education as the Practice of Freedom: Paulo Freire and the Promise of Critical Pedagogy. *Policy Futures in Education,* 8(6), pp. 715–721.

Goodley, D. (2016). *Disability Studies: An Interdisciplinary Introduction.* London: SAGE Publications.

Greene, R. W. (2014). *Lost at School: Why Our Kids with Behavioral Challenges Are Falling through the Cracks and How We Can Help Them.* Simon and Schuster.

Gu, Q., and Day, C. (2013). Challenges to Teacher Resilience: Conditions Count. *British Educational Research Journal,* 39(1), pp. 22–44.

Halford, J.M. (1998), *Easing the way for new teachers,* Educational Leadership, Vol. 55 No. 5, pp. 33–36.

Hooks, b. (2003). *Teaching Community: A Pedagogy of Hope* (Vol. 36). Psychology Press.

Ingersoll, R. and Merrill, E. (2012), *Seven trends: the transformation of the teaching force,* Consortium for Policy Research in Education Working Paper (#WP-01), University of Pennsylvania, 1 November.

Jaffee, A., and Casey, Z. A. (2020). Chapter 92 White Supremacy. In: *Encyclopedia of Critical Whiteness Studies in Education.* Leiden, The Netherlands: Brill. Available at: https://doi-org.proxy.library.nyu.edu/10.1163/9789004444836_092 [Accessed 8/26/24]

Kendi, I. X. (2023). *How to Be an Antiracist.* London: Oneworld.

Ladson-Billings, G. (2014). Culturally Relevant Pedagogy 2.0: aka the Remix. *Harvard Educational Review,* 84(1), pp. 74–84.

Lorde, A. (1997). Age, Race, Class, and Sex: Women Redefining Difference. *Cultural Politics,* 11, pp. 374–380.

Love, B. (2019). *We Want to Do More Than Survive: Abolitionist Teaching and the Pursuit of Educational Justice.* Boston: Beacon Press.

Love, B. L. (2023). *Punished for Dreaming: How School Reform Harms Black Children and How We Heal*. New York: St. Martin's Press.

Mansfield, C., Beltman, S., Broadley, T., and Weatherby-Fell, N. (2016). Building Resilience in Teacher Education: An Evidenced Informed Framework. *Teaching and Teacher Education,* 54, pp. 77–87.

McKimmie, J., Allen, J., and Tennant, M. C. (2019). Teacher Resilience: A Review of the Literature. *Educational Psychology Review,* 31(2), pp. 301–323.

Moir, E. (2016). New Teacher Development for Every Inning. *New Teacher Center.* https://digitalbell-bucket.s3.amazonaws.com/C0F6D633-5056-907D-8D2A-631AF4C842AF.pdf

Muhammad, G. (2023). *Unearthing Joy: A Guide to Culturally and Historically Responsive Curriculum and Instruction*. Scholastic.

Naraian, S. (2016). Teaching for "Real" Reconciling Explicit Literacy Instruction with Inclusive Pedagogy in a Fourth-Grade Urban Classroom. *Urban Education,* 54(10), pp. 1581–1607. Available at: https://doi.org/10.1177/0042085916648742. [Accessed 8/26/24]

Naraian, S., and Schlessinger, S. (2018). Becoming an Inclusive Educator: Agentive Maneuverings in a Collaboratively Taught Classroom. *Teaching and Teacher Education,* 71, pp. 179–189. https://doi.org/10.1016/j.tate.2017.12.012

Naraian, S., and Schlessinger, S. (2021). *Narratives of Inclusive Teaching: Stories of Becoming in the Field*. New York: Peter Lang.

Oyler, C. (2011). Teacher Preparation for Inclusive and Critical (Special) Education. *Teacher Education and Special Education,* 34(3), pp. 201–218.

Oyler, C. (2017). *Learning to Teach Inclusively: Student Teachers' Classroom Inquiries*. Routledge.

Pantić, N. (2015). A Model for Study of Teacher Agency for Social Justice. *Teachers and Teaching,* 21(6), pp. 759–778.

Paris, D., and Alim, H. S. eds. (2017). *Culturally Sustaining Pedagogies: Teaching and Learning for Justice in a Changing World*. New York: Teachers College Press.

Sapon-Shevin, M. (2010). *Because We Can Change the World: A Practical Guide to Building Cooperative, Inclusive Classroom Communities*. Corwin Press.

Sawyer, K. E. (2011). *Creativity for Educators*. New York: Teachers College Press.

Schlessinger, S. L. (2018). Reclaiming Teacher Intellectualism through and for Inclusive Education. *International Journal of Inclusive Education,* 22(3), pp. 268–284.

Schlessinger, S.L., and Oyler, C. (in press). Inclusive Teacher Preparation. In: M. and T. Winn, eds., *Encyclopedia for Social Justice*. Bloomsbury.

Sensoy, O., and DiAngelo, R. (2017). *Is Everyone Really Equal?: An Introduction to Key Concepts in Social Justice Education*. New York: Teachers College Press.

Shor, I. (1996). *When Students Have Power: Negotiating Authority in a Critical Pedagogy*. Chicago: University of Chicago Press.

Slee, R. (2013). Meeting Some Challenges of Inclusive Education in an Age of Exclusion. *Asian Journal of Inclusive Education,* 1(2), pp. 3–17.

Sleeter, C., and Carmona, J. F. (2017). *Un-standardizing Curriculum: Multicultural Teaching in the Based Classroom*. New York: Teachers College Press.

Sutcher, L., Darling-Hammond, L. and Carver-Thomas, D. (2016), Coming Crisis in Teaching? Teacher Supply, Demand, and Shortages in the U.S, research brief, Learning Policy Institute, Palo Alto, CA.

Sue, D. W., and Spanierman, L. (2020). *Microaggressions in Everyday Life*. John Wiley & Sons.

Tatum, B. D. (2017). *Why Are All the Black Kids Sitting Together in the Cafeteria?: And Other Conversations about Race*. Hachette UK.

Taubman, P. M. (2010). *Teaching by Numbers: Deconstructing the Discourse of Standards and Accountability in Education*. Routledge.

Taylor, S. J. (2004). Caught in the Continuum: A Critical Analysis of the Principle of the Least Restrictive Environment. *Research and Practice for Persons with Severe Disabilities,* 29(4), pp. 218–230.

Teachers College, Columbia University. (n.d.). *Black Paint Curriculum Lab: About*. Available at: www.tc.columbia.edu/black-paint-curriculum-lab/ [Accessed April 15, 2024].

Trinter, C. P., and Hughes, H. E. (2021). Teachers as Curriculum Designers: Inviting Teachers into the Productive Struggle. *RMLE Online,* 44(3), pp. 1–16.

Valenzuela, A. (2010). *Subtractive Schooling: US-Mexican Youth and the Politics of Caring*. 3rd ed. Albany: SUNY Press.

Valle, J. W., and Connor, D. J. (2019). *Rethinking Disability: A Disability Studies Approach to Inclusive Practices*. Routledge.

Varenne, H., and McDermottt, R. (2018). *Successful Failure: The School America Builds*. Routledge.

Waitoller, F. R., and Artiles, A. J. (2013). A Decade of Professional Development Research for Inclusive Education: A Critical Review and Notes for a Research Program. *Review of Educational Research,* 83(3), pp. 319–356.

Walker, D. F., and Soltis, J. F. (2004). *Curriculum and Aims*. New York: Teachers College Press.

Weinstein, C. S., Tomlinson, C. A., and Jolliff, G. (2018). *How to Meet Individual Needs: Differentiating Instruction in Responsive Classrooms*. 3rd ed. ASCD.

Wiggins, G., & McTighe, J. (2011). The Understanding by Design guide to creating high-quality units. ASCD.

Index

ableism. 11, 13–14, 18, 21, 27, 95, 98, 104, 108
active listening. 55–57
advocacy. 35–36
affinity groups. 110
Aguilar, E.. 38
American schooling structures. 21
Annamma, S. A.. 13
Anyon, J.. 4
Artiles, A. J.. 8
"attitude toward teaching" curve. 108
audit culture. 67, 85, 86, 87, 102

behavioral skills. 22
benchmark assessments. 24, 31, 71
best practices. 100, 103
Billings, G. L.. 4
Black American History. 46
boredom. 68, 78

civil rights movement. 46, 77, 78–79, 80

collaborative learning. 52
Collaborative Team Teaching (CTT). 5, 7
commitments. 61; actions from reflections, for change. 36–38; building resilience from. 39–41; contextualized. 22–36; educational theories and frameworks. 26–28; reflection from. 27–28; for social-justice-oriented educators. 17–18; social justice-oriented educator. 19; social model of disability framework. 17, 20; social-justice-oriented educators. 38; to power of community. 60; to teaching for social justice and inclusivity. 18–22; Universal Design for Learning (UDL) framework. 21–22; to your Self. 38–39
communities. 93–111, *see also* Loving Learning Communities; bridging racial discrepancy students. 96–97; engaging with, absence of. 95–96; having each other, sense of. 97–100; intellectual, skilled, and autonomous teachers. 102–104; ostracized educators. 93–95; positive

classroom. 22; professional development opportunities. 100–102; Teachers College Inclusive Classroom Project. *see* Teachers College Inclusive Classroom Project (TCICP)

Connor, D. J.. 17

consultants. 50, 58, 61, 101, 107

co-teaching and co-planning inquiry team. 106

creative and responsive curricular change. 84–87

creativity. 90, 100; creative intellectual. 84–87; strategic. 84

Critical Friends Groups. 111

critical pedagogy. 4

Critical Race Theory (CRT). 26–28, 30, 31, 33, 35, 40, 94

critical thinking skills. 67

culturally relevant pedagogy. 4, 106

culturally responsive pedagogy. 4, 54, 94

curricular play; civil rights movement, test prep unit. 77–80; creative and responsive curricular change. 84–87; methods for. 86–87; purpose of. 85–86; curricular extension. 90–92; design engaging learning experiences. 78–79; different hidden curriculum. 80–84; practices developed for. 89–90; standardized testing and auditing in. 67–68; student resistance, power and capacity recognition. 80–84; student voice, creative risks for centering. 75–80; student-centered and emotionally supportive curriculum; case studies in. 70–75; data usage in. 70–75; teacher resilience through. 87–88; testing season, impacts of. 67–68

curriculum. 65–68; analysis of. 89; designing. 85, 87; hidden. 80–84, 87, 89; responsive history. 97; social justice-oriented. 85; student-centered and emotionally supportive. 70–75

data, significance of. 62, 89

dehumanization. 94, 97, 110

Deliovsky, K.. 13

differences, embracing. 44–48

digital tools. 83

Dirkswager, E. J.. 88

disabilities; deficit models. 29, 36; as difference. 6–7; high incidence. 6; social model. 17, 20

Disability Critical Race Theory (DisCrit). 26–28, 30, 31, 33, 35, 40

Disability Studies in Education (DSE). 7, 27, 28, 30, 31, 33, 35, 94

discrimination. 13, 35

disempowered teachers. 25

documentation, significance of. 62, 89

Drew, S. V.. 10

educational theories and frameworks; Critical Race Theory. 26–28; Disability Critical Race Theory. 26–28; Disability Studies in Education. 26–28; reflection from; advocating students. 35–36; assessments and learning outcomes. 30–31; classroom community. 31–33; curriculum design. 28–30; role of power. 33–35

end-of-day sifting. 62

environmental barriers, mitigating. 29

equality in education. 1–2

expert team facilitator. 103

Farris-Berg, K.. 88

feedback documentation. 89

Ferguson, A. A.. 6

Freire, P.. 4

futility, feeling of. 25, 36, 37

Gay, G.. 4

Giroux, H.. 4

hidden curriculum. 80–84, 87, 89

hierarchies, disruption of. 48–53

idealism. 34, 39, 41

implicit bias. 34, 38

inclusionism. 8

inclusive classroom learning. 74

inclusive education. 7–8

inclusive teaching. 20

Individualized Education Programs (IEPs). 71, 84, 86

inquiry teams. 101, 105, 107, 108

integrated co-teaching model. 22–23, 69, 80

investigation, significance of. 40

isolation. 94, 110

Kendi, I. X.. 17

labeling; and disability. 8, 20, 21, 23, 35, 51; and race. 95

listening to students. 53–54

literacy supports inquiry team. 106

love, trust, and vulnerability in classroom. 44–63, 110; disrupting hierarchies and sharing power. 48–53; embracing differences. 44–48; fostering resilience through. 59–63; listening beyond morning meeting. 58; listening to students. 53–54; responsive listening and action. 57–58; teachers active listening. 55–57

Loving Learning Communities. *see also* communities; curricular extension. 112–13; for resilience. 109–11

McClaren, P.. 4

metaphysical barrier of whiteness. 21

microaggressions. 13, 94

Moir, E.. 108

Morningside Center for Teaching Social Responsibility. 33

multimodal inquiry team. 105

negative stereotypes. 95

Nusbaum, E.. 6

oppression. 4, 13

policy reforms, audit culture-driven. 85

positive classroom community. 22

possibilities; being open to. 61; identification of. 61–62, 63

power; role of. 33–35; sharing. 48–53

professional development (PD). 100–02, 103, 104, 110, *see also* Teachers College Inclusive Classroom Project (TCICP)

racial disproportionality, in special education. 6–7, 20–21

racial diversity. 1

racism. 17, 18, 21, 27, 95

reflection, significance of. 40–41

reflective practices. 38

relationships. 109

resources; collection of. 39; digital. 90; refinement of. 39

Responsive Classroom resources. 33

responsive history curriculum. 97

responsive listening and action. 57–58, 59, 62, 63

restorative justice inquiry team. 106

restrictive environments. 51, 70

Rethinking Schools. 111

Rose, D.. 5

self-care. 38–39, 41

self-compassion. 38

shared experiences. 111

social justice-oriented education and inclusive teaching; building love, trusty relationships in classroom. 17–19; commitments to. 17–19; community. 93–111; curricular play. 65–90

social justice-oriented prescribed curriculum. 85

social-emotional development and support. 69–75

societal barriers, mitigating. 29

socio-economic diversity. 1

Soltis, J. F.. 65

Sosnowski, C.. 10

special education. 6–7, 20–21, 94, 100, 101, 106

Special Education Teacher Support Services (SETSS). 80

stereotypes. 95, 97

structural racism. 18, 98

struggles faced by a teacher. 8–9

student identities, differences in. 45

student teachers. 17, 20, 27

student-centered and emotionally supportive curriculum. 70–75

taken-for-granted practices. 19

teacher education programs. 17, 18

Teachers College Inclusive Classroom Project (TCICP). 100–02, 105; learning in loving community. 107–09; own work in field, articulating. 106–07; research in field, knowing. 105–06; work sharing with the field. 107

Tomlinson, C.. 5

traditional classroom management. 52

Universal Design for Learning (UDL) framework. 5, 21–22, 94, 106

Valle, J. W.. 17

Waitoller, F. R.. 8

Walker, D. F.. 65

White supremacy. 5, 11, 12–13, 95

xenophobia. 18

www.ingramcontent.com/pod-product-compliance
Lightning Source LLC
Chambersburg PA
CBHW060838190426
43197CB00040B/2672